FUTURE

Commo

of the

Carla Heslop (2017)

<u>carlaheslop@slingshot.co.nz</u>

ISBN 9781973198819

INTRODUCTION

This book is the third of three booklets summarizing my research into 3 questions: Why are we here? What's it all about? Where are we heading? At the end of each booklet there is also a Recommended Reading list of the most interesting books sourced for this info.

Past Life Lessons
- *Lessons from Regression* – 35 common themes from past-life regressions reported across the research
- *Personal Stories* of reincarnation
- *Soulmates*
- *A Universal Plan*

Past Life Answers
- *Additional Insights from a Workshop with Brian Weiss,* (Sydney, 2011), which expands on some of the common themes outlined in *Lessons*
- *Questions and Answers* further explaining these themes with additional examples from the research

Future Visions
- *Common Visions of the Future*
  Findings from studies of near-death experiences (NDEs) future-life progressions, Nostradamus and Cayce
- *Catastrophe and Spiritual Awakening Linked*
- *Two Possible Timelines* for the future – maybe more
- *Our Destiny*

CONTENTS

WINTER IS COMING!

While the message of the New Age seems to be to "live in the now," there is no doubt that it presents a challenge to the human psyche. This is epitomized in the moral of the ant and the grasshopper. The grasshopper, you might remember, spent the summer singing and dancing with no thought of the future, but the clever ant took note of the seasons and stock market trends. Predicting hard times ahead, he stocked up the pantry. When winter came, his family had plenty while the grasshopper went begging. The message is that the wise person plans for the future.

I don't just mean insurance plans, savings plans and Christmas Club plans. We're a global community now. We've become aware that activities on the other side of the world can affect the quality of our own lives; and we know that while these problems may not touch us right now, sooner or later they will impact on everyone. Having a full larder and a portfolio of stocks won't help us. When it comes to the really big issues – pollution, global warming, earth upheavals – the ants and grasshoppers of humanity will all be in the same boat.

This might be hard to get too bothered about while the sun is shining, but the warning signs of autumn are already happening. We need to know what effects these crises and changes will have on us and what we, as individuals aware of our united spiritual identity, can do about them. In this section, we'll be looking at common visions of the future and how the wise man or woman can prepare for the world ahead.

TWO WEIRD EXPERIENCES

Long before I began this research into future visions there were two occasions in my life when I 'saw' my future self. Both were in the short-term future and felt very strange.

Visualization technique (around 7 weeks)
The first was almost 30 years ago when my daughter was 5. She had had intermittent hearing problems without any apparent cause, and I'd been told she would probably grow out of it. However, her teacher felt her learning would be impeded and I needed to "do something about it." At that time, the popular (in fact the only) solution was grommets (tubes) inserted in the eardrum to drain fluid from the ear. Our foster child, also 5, had them; they caused ear infections whenever the ear got wet and permanent scarring of the eardrum once they were removed. It wasn't an option.

I had recently learned about the technique of visualization – repeated imaging of a desired outcome until it manifested and read about its successes in sport and healing, so I decided to try it. As my daughter had just failed her last hearing test, I imagined a scenario of her again being taken through a test, earphones etc, with the hearing-test lady ultimately saying, "Well done, Eloise. You've passed your hearing test;" and then coming over to where I was sitting and saying, "Your daughter has passed her hearing test, Mrs Heslop. She doesn't have a hearing problem."

I arranged to do this with a friend who had his own goal, and we spent half an hour every evening, 5 days a week, each visualizing our own scenarios over and over. I wasn't sure if I believed in it, but I had nothing to lose!

One day, about 6 weeks later, I was ambushed at school by the principal and my daughter's teacher who informed me that they had arranged for a lady from the health department to come and test my daughter's ears. It was clear that since I wasn't taking action, they were going to force the issue. (I hadn't told them I was visualizing a solution!)

We proceeded to the staffroom where a hearing test was set up. I sat to the side practising my 'I'm not having my daughter's ear drums operated on' speech. After a while, I dimly heard the hearing test lady say, "Well done, Eloise. You've passed your hearing test." Then she came over to me and said, "Your daughter has passed her hearing test, Mrs Heslop. She doesn't have a hearing problem." The exact words!

It wasn't until the end of that sentence that I realized I was in the future I had imagined – the hearing test, the setting, the people. It was a very freaky experience, but my daughter's hearing problem was a thing of the past from that moment.

(My friend's goal was to meet the love of his life. At about the same time as my visualization came true, he met a young woman at his dancing class who he married a few years later.)

Silva Mind Control technique (almost instantaneous)
The second time I saw the future was just as odd. I have always been fascinated by the idea that we only use 10% of our faculties. It seems such a waste. One day, I came across *The Silva Mind Control Method (1977),* by Jose Silva. In it, he offers a number of ways to add to that percentage.

Silva had noted that when people mentally review their past, their eyes travel to the right and when they look to the future, their eyes travel to the left. He utilized this in an intriguing technique for finding a lost object. Reading about this late one night, I decided to try it. His instructions were to get into a relaxed (alpha) state. Once there, you visualise a blank screen and on that screen create a picture of the object as you last saw it, in as much detail as you can.

When you feel that this image has been imprinted on your mind, move that screen away to the right (the past) and slide a

7

new screen into your mental visual field from the left (the future). Hold the idea of the lost object in mind (without attempting to create any visual pictures) and wait patiently until a picture forms on the screen.

A couple of months earlier I had lost the adaptor that allowed me to fit the small prong at the end of my microphone cord into the larger aperture of my cassette tape recorder. (It was the nineties!) This adaptor looked like a large bullet about 8 cm (3 inches) long with a hole at one end for the microphone prong. I had looked everywhere for it, particularly in my living room as that was where I last remembered it – behind cushions, down the back of my couch, even tipping my armchairs upside down. No stone had been left unturned.

Anyway, I closed my eyes and visualised the adaptor on my mental screen, in detail, for about 5 minutes. Satisfied, I mentally pulled that screen down to the right and pulled a new screen (sort of like a whiteboard) in from the left. And waited. At first, I saw nothing. And at second... and third! But I was in bed, not going anywhere, nothing better to do, when a scene formed on the screen.

I saw myself in my living room reaching down the side of the cushion on the armchair by my front door, fossicking around and pulling out the adaptor, holding it up in front of me and looking at it – probably, I imagined, with a feeling of satisfaction.

I have to say I was quite dashed and a bit annoyed. I'd already looked down the side of that chair – more than once – and no adaptor had been forthcoming. Humph!

Three days later, I was in the family room about to head off to bed when I decided to have one last look for that adaptor. I did some more tipping over of my couch and armchairs. I fossicked down the backs of cushions and down the sides of seats. The last place I looked was the armchair by the door. I nearly wasn't going to; I knew I was wasting my time, but I reached down the side of the cushion and fossicked around anyway. I felt something long and round. Next thing I knew, I was pulling out that adaptor.

I couldn't believe my eyes. I held it out in front of me and stared at it. Just as I'd seen myself do on the screen in my mind. However, the emotion I was experiencing wasn't satisfaction; it was astonishment. "I don't believe it," I said to myself. "I don't believe it!" And yet it was true. Three nights previously, I had seen the future!

The effect of my first experience of the future was to open my mind to the realization that our thoughts have power. In some inexplicable way, consciousness creates, and we can have an effect on our future reality. This ability is alluded to in the messages of at least 3 of my sources. The effect of the second experience was to make me realize that the limits of our awareness stretch beyond the boundaries of time and space. It also stretched the limits of my own belief system at the time. Why had all my years studying psychology never mentioned any of this stuff? How is it even possible?

I had yet to find out that as well as the subconscious, there is another level of mind of which most of us are largely unaware: the superconscious or higher self that is part the universal mind that unites us all.

HOW IS IT POSSIBLE TO SEE THE PAST AND THE FUTURE?

It's challenging enough to get your head around the idea that people can revisit their past lives. But how can they see something that hasn't even happened yet? It seems we have faculties, as yet undeveloped in most of us, which enable us to access future potentialities. The closest analogy in our 3D world is that of a person in a plane directing the driver of a car below on the road he is to travel. The person in the plane (higher self/superconscious) can see the road previously travelled and the road far ahead, as well as alternative routes, but the driver of the car (earthly consciousness) can only see the road immediately in front of him. The alternative routes can be compared to the choices we make on our life path.

Past Lives, Future Lives

Someone who could see the road both before and beyond the present day is Jenny Cockell, a British housewife who recalled snatches of past lives all through her childhood and found the phenomenon so natural that she thought that everybody did it. Her story became famous when her persistent desire to find out what had happened to the children she left behind in a previous life in post-WWI Ireland led her to seek them out.

She ultimately became reunited with several of them (all much older than herself in this current life), who have acknowledged her as their past-life mother. Her story has been featured in a British TV documentary and dramatized on U.S. television, *Yesterday's Children (2000),* starring Jane Seymour.

The really interesting part of Jenny's story is that this wasn't the only past-life she recalled, or even her most recent past-life. She spontaneously recalled several more past lives and some future lives! As an adult she undertook hypnotherapy to find out more about them. She likens reincarnation to a series of jobs in different cities, each with its own challenge and potential for growth.

Here are the ones she remembers in her book *Past Lives, Future Lives (1998)*:

800   *Effan, a Welsh villager whose 2 children died of smallpox*

1223   *Gwen, daughter of a trader, probably British, whose brothers had just returned from the Crusades*

1500   *A small boy in a Tudor house who died young*

1650   *Son of a carpenter, deaf or autistic*

1709-1760 *Anna, daughter of impoverished French farmers, sold young as a servant – a life of squalor and poverty reflective of the conditions just before the French Revolution*

1830   *Dockyard waif (female) who died of starvation. Companion of that time is present-day husband, Steve*

1850   *Japanese girl from a wealthy family, drowned as a teenager on a boat-trip to an arranged marriage with a much older man which she was reluctant to go through with*

1895-1932 *Mary Sutton, a poor Irish mother who died in childbirth, leaving her 8 children to the care of her drunkard husband. (This life was the subject of her book, Yesterday's Children, also named Across Time and Death)*

1940-1945 *Charles, died young of a fever*

1953-   *Jenny Cockell, her current life as an English chiropodist (foot doctor), wife, mother, researcher, writer*

11

2040   *Nadia, a Nepalese village girl – a relatively happy life although her first child died young*

2150   *A Polish woman, same husband as today, living in conditions of hardship and poverty*

2228   *Janice – a Unichem technician taking samples of plants in South America for possible medical or textile uses.*

In this life, Middle America is fairly empty of people (possibly due to flooding). Most of the population is along the coast; however, the oceans are still too polluted to fish.

2285   *Sheryl – an American teenager. There are many fewer people than now, but there is a general atmosphere of security about conditions of the day. Environmental considerations are very important. Chemical pollution of soil and water (and hence the food chain) had reduced fertility in all animals including humans.*

Jenny offers three interesting glimpses of the future as well as a noteworthy indication of shorter gaps between lives.

THERAPISTS, VISIONARIES, NDErS

Throughout history, there are records of people who have had visions of the future – prophets, seers, oracles, shamans, sibyls, witches, clairvoyants and psychics. There are so many names for them the phenomenon is clearly not that uncommon. These people are not like the futurists of today – scientists and philosophers who study sociological, technological and economic trends and make predictions. Rather, they are able to tap into a different source, the invisible realm variously called the universal mind, the superconscious, or the Akashic Record (described by some as the universe's super-computer). People who have 'seen' the future report curious and sometimes terrifying similarities in their visions.

In order to get a comprehensive picture of the future, I have examined findings from three completely different fields: future-life-progression hypnotherapy, which has been sitting quietly in the background for almost as long as we have been aware of past-life-regression therapy; the field of near-death experiences (NDEs), which has been extensively researched; and two renowned prophets from the past: Edgar Cayce and Nostradamus. All provide thought-provoking scenarios of possible futures that have implications for us all.

Future Life Progression (FLP) Therapists

Brian Weiss: As with his 'discovery' of past life regression therapy in the 1980s (when a client under hypnosis brought up past-life experiences), in the new millennium, Dr. Brian Weiss noted that clients were starting to spontaneously 'jump ahead' to future-life experiences and, what's more, finding it beneficial. Many of his clients' visions of their near future in this lifetime have proven to be true.

Weiss found some fascinating commonalities in people's future experiences and began to conduct seminars in which he takes his groups on journeys into the future: 100 years, 500 years and 1000 years from now. His seminar attendees at the time of publishing his book, *Same Soul, Many Bodies,* in 2004 numbered over 2000 and there is a consensus on their visions of the future.

Anne Jirsch: A U.K.-based pioneer of future-life progression (FLP), Jirsch runs the only training school for FLP in the world with 250 practitioners in eight countries. Originally a psychic/clairvoyant, she trained in hypnotherapy and past-life regression, later stumbling upon future-life progressions by having clients spontaneously jump ahead to a future life.

As with Weiss, the aim of Jirsch's research is to guide us in our choices today so we can create our own best future thus contributing to humanity's best future as well. Knowing possible outcomes of today's decisions means that we can live the optimal plan for our lives. **We can learn and grow without suffering** by connecting with our future selves and being told where we've got it wrong and how to change.

According to Jirsch's research with her clients, there seems to be 4 main paths that our lives can take, and sometimes we switch between these paths depending on our current choices. These in turn will affect future lifetimes.

In her book, *The Future is Yours (2007),* as well as providing a number of visualization techniques to allow readers to train themselves to contact their future lifetimes, she offers information from her own future-life progressions. Of greater interest, she collates the results of a worldwide study she conducted of her clients and followers, (including participants in Australia and N.Z.) by asking them to follow a guided visualization to progress to the future and then answer a list of questions about their experiences and what they noticed 20, 50 and 100 years into the future. While part of the study was conducted in workshops, the majority of the questionnaires were answered individually. There were many common features in these future visions.

Helen Wambach, Ph.D. (1925-1986): Originally a disbeliever in reincarnation, psychologist Wambach was one of the earliest scientific researchers into past lives. Like Weiss, she found that under hypnosis some of her subjects automatically jumped ahead to future lives. But what they saw was so disturbing – a devastated and depopulated world – that throughout the early 1980s, she and associates Leo Sprinkle and Chet Snow, (both PhDs), conducted dozens of group workshops across America and France, resulting in nearly four hundred future-life progressions. They published the results of this massive exercise in *Mass Dreams of the Future: Group Progressions to the Twenty-Second and Twenty-Fourth Centuries (1989)*. Of the 2500 people in the study, only 6 percent reported being alive in 2100 A.D. and 13 percent in 2300 A.D. Evidence, Dr. Wambach believed, of a decline of up to 95% of the population within a few generations.

Dolores Cannon (1931-2014): A past-life regressionist since 1979, specializing in the recovery and cataloguing of Lost Knowledge, Cannon taught and lectured all over the world. Also a prolific and best-selling author, I've taken findings largely from her intriguing *Conversations With Nostradamus, Vol. 2, (1992)* and her penultimate book, *The Three Waves of Volunteers and the New Earth (2011)*.

Visionaries

I have also included predictions/ prophecies from two of the most famous clairvoyants of all time. **Edgar Cayce** (1877-1945), called The Sleeping Prophet, answered many questions put to him about the past, future and the meaning of life while in a self-induced hypnotic trance. These thousands of readings for people from all walks of life have been recorded and are universally available through his Association for Research and Enlightenment, A.R.E.

No discussion of prophecy would be complete without a mention of **Nostradamus**. While a lot has been written about

Nostradamus, much of it has not been validated. Nostradamus was a clever 16th century physician and seer renowned for writing a series of books containing, in total, almost 1000 quatrains (4-line poems) in obscure language purporting to be predictions of the future. The obscurity of his prophecies is said to be due to the Inquisition's fervor for torturing and burning witches. Possibly for the same reason, he preferred not to be called a prophet.

Nostradamus travelled the (known) world for knowledge and also saw visions of the future in a large obsidian mirror. This is where he obtained knowledge of some of his cures – which were largely based on dietary and hygiene considerations at odds with the day. For a time he was under the protection of Catherine de Medici, Queen of France, who had a keen interest in his prophetic powers as he had predicted – correctly – that three of her sons would be kings.

I didn't originally intend to include anything by Nostradamus as his quatrains, although famous, are generally agreed to be too obscure to be of any worth. However, past-life regression therapist Dolores Cannon was enabled to decipher his material after regressing a client who was a student of Nostradamus's in the 1500s. Through this subject and others, she was able to have conversations with Nostradamus (and made this the title of a series of books explaining his visions of the future).

The predictions I have included come from *Conversations with Nostradamus, Volume 2 (1992)* and a two-hour YouTube video of Cannon talking in 2012 about her contact with Nostradamus in 1987 and how she came to translate the Nostradamus prophecies for the world.

Nostradamus informed her subject, under regression, that he had been looking for a means to communicate with the people of our time as he had seen that, in the future, his prophecies weren't being understood and thus weren't helping mankind prepare for the disasters to come. He had foreseen some very dark times and he was concerned that if people didn't know the worst that could happen, they wouldn't be able to prevent it. The time he had seen for these terrible things (e.g. WW3) was starting so it was crucial that people know about them.

Nostradamus was willing to help her translate and explain the quatrains which he wrote to describe his visions, but there were difficulties with concepts – Nostradamus had to use 16th century language to describe some future developments he saw. Also, Nostradamus was sometimes impatient with Dolores's limited knowledge of the classics, which was the mark of a well-educated person in his time.

Many of Nostradamus's quatrains use classical or mythological allusions, not to mention references to countries by their ancient names. He also used anagrams and other literary devices to obscure his writing so as not to be obvious in his future predictions in order to further avoid accusations of witchcraft. E.g. Old Greek names were used for countries in the Middle East. Hermes or Mercury referred to communication. Vulcan was a reference to war. Vestal virgins, who tended the eternal flame, referred to the atomic bomb.

Throughout her two or three years' contact with Nostradamus, Dolores had altogether 12 subjects through whom he 'spoke.' As all reported similar messages she felt it was good proof of the reliability of the information she was getting.

Nostradamus told one regression subject that he could sense Dolores as 'an energy.' He described his contact with her as 'being in the realm of limbo' and was astonished to discover she was a woman, as women in his time were uneducated and it was clear he had a low opinion of them! (He also mentioned that as well as Dolores and her subject John, through whom she was communicating, he had other 'spirits' come through from the 23rd century.)

Deciphering the quatrains enabled Cannon to get an overall picture of the future Nostradamus had foreseen, which she describes on YouTube. Nostradamus told Dolores that people could prevent these terrible events through the power of their minds focusing on the opposite and that she needed to tell the world this.

Near-Death Experiencers

The NDErs I quote below were chosen for the detail of their prophecies. I also mention several others who can be found, amongst many more, on NDE researcher Kevin William's website: www.near-death.com/science/research/future.html. Williams has summarized prophecies of future events from people who were either told about them by beings on the other side or shown visions during their near-death experiences (NDEs).

Dannion Brinkley was a black ops soldier in the American military before his first NDE in 1975, when he was struck by lightning. After a shattering life review on the other side, he changed his life and began to devote his time to ministering to the dying and to a volunteer hospice group, The Twilight Brigade, which he founded in 1984. He has received numerous awards for his work and written three books about his near-death experiences, *Saved by the Light (1994), At Peace in the Light (1995)* and *Secrets of the Light (2008).*

During his first NDE, Brinkley was shown 100 visions of the future in 'boxes of knowledge.' He was shown famine, war, environmental destruction, man-made disease, chip implantation, and financial manipulations leading to an astronomical rise in the price of gas. He also saw the future of medicine moving into non-invasive light therapies "for stress reduction in the centers [he] was sent back to build."

Diagnosed with terminal brain cancer, **Mellen-Thomas Benedict** (1949-2017) had a 90-minute NDE in 1982 during which he met a Being of Light (our 'Higher Self Matrix') and was shown the nature of the universe and the importance and relevance of every single individual before he returned to life cured! During his NDE, Mellen-Thomas learned that what you believe is what you experience – but not always in an obvious way. He learned that everything is made of energy, of light, of God – there is no separation. After his NDE, he was able to revisit the 'Light' at will and, like a number of other NDErs, brought back some amazing discoveries, in particular Phototherapy, in which sick cells within the body are stimulated by light in order to return to optimal health. He has been extensively studied and a 7-page PDF of his NDE, *Journey Through the Light and Back,* is available on the web.

Ned Dougherty, *(Fast Lane to Heaven, 2001)*, a self-centered atheist, night-club owner, alcoholic and materialist at the time of his NDE in 1984, somebody quite different in the years following, was in his mid-30s when a heart attack stopped him in his tracks! During the NDE which followed, he became aware of his mission in life, which was to embark upon charitable and missionary work. A wonderful 'Lady of Light' (whom he identified as the Virgin Mary) revealed to him future global catastrophes, many of which have since occurred.

Dougherty, a lapsed Catholic, was also told that his earthly cravings, which had taken such a negative turn, had actually been intended to lead him in the search for a spiritual path to satisfy them. After his NDE, Dougherty went on to become a spokesperson and board member of the National Association for Near Death Studies. He also created his non-profit organization, Mission of Angels, collecting reports of spiritual experiences, and worked to create a new community of spiritually-minded people.

Prior to his NDE, **Howard Storm** was an art professor at North Kentucky University and an atheist. After his NDE in 1985 due to a perforated stomach, he changed the course of his life, resigning his university position, attending a theological seminary and becoming a minister. Because of his concern for the future, he was given quite a bit of information concerning it; in particular, a vision of what life on Earth will be like in 200 years. He describes his experiences in his book, *My Descent into Death (2005).*

Other sources

I also quote from various other sources which, despite their diversity, foretell or confirm future scenarios with sometimes startling similarity.

Of note in this section is **Bruce Moen**, (*Voyages into the Afterlife, 1999*), an engineer who was trained to experience out-of-body journeys into the afterlife during meditation. His technique was developed by Robert Monroe, founder of The Monroe Institute, to whom OBEs (out-of-body experiences) happened spontaneously, taking him to new levels of consciousness a.k.a. the afterlife. It seems there are a number of levels, or planes, in the afterlife depending on your vibration or level of spiritual awareness.

As with NDErs, Moen met and spoke with people on 'the other side' who were helping mankind's development behind the scenes. He was told that humans as a group want to know more about their existence beyond the physical as this is their destiny. This is why more people are having experiences of the afterlife. He was also assured that his desire to write a book to let people know about his experiences would come to pass. (Moen has had 5 books published and now conducts workshops on astral travel worldwide.) He specifically asked about the 'Big Plan for the Earth.'

While some sources describe a very grim view of mankind's future, others, in particular Anne Jirsch and Mellen-Thomas Benedict, are more hopeful. All foresee big changes.

COMMON FEATURES OF THE NEAR-DEATH EXPERIENCE

In 1975 when Raymond Moody's book, *Life After Life: The Investigation of a Phenomenon – Survival of Bodily Death,* first came out summarizing 50 cases of people who had 'died' and been resuscitated, it was big news and quite controversial. However, these days the near-death experience is an accepted field of scientific study and, as it says in the preface of his latest edition, it has helped form our modern expectations of what we will experience after death.

NDEs provide information about the afterlife – or, actually, the interlife because we now know that our spirit or consciousness doesn't stop there and put its feet up, but is born again in a new body. So what have researchers found in the decades since Moody published? Pretty much what Moody found, only more of it! Thousands of cases have now been studied and most of the subjects report at least 7 of the 12 features common to the NDE phenomenon. Some subjects have incredibly detailed experiences (generally those who were 'dead' longer) while a few are just fleeting.

Common Features of Near Death Experiences (NDEs)

1. **An OBE (Out of Body Experience)** – separation of consciousness from the physical body. Some subjects have described floating out of their body, seeing doctors working on their bodies to resuscitate them, feeling anxiety or pity for the body, not recognizing it as theirs, or feeling disgust or detachment from it. Others report being able to travel anywhere. (For example, a woman who was rushed to hospital with a heart attack died and left her body. After being resuscitated, she told how she saw a man's tennis shoe on the ledge of a third-storey window, invisible from the ground. When the shoe was later found, the woman's description was correct in every detail.) Some subjects

were 'dead' for a far greater period than the accepted time for healthy resuscitation (7 minutes for brain function to be re-established). For example, Mary Neal was under water for at least twice that time. In her out-of-body state Mary remembers one bystander suggesting they cease attempts to resuscitate her body (bloated from oxygen starvation) as she would be a vegetable. Nevertheless, Mary survived to continue her career as an orthopedic (spinal) surgeon, write her book, *To Heaven and Back (2012),* and make other notable contributions to society and the environment.

2. **Passing through a tunnel,** void, or passageway; one subject described it as a valley and compared it to 'the valley of the shadow of death.'

3. **Heightened sensory experience**. Everything is brighter, blind NDErs can see, things far away can be seen as clearly as those close up; and all reported that they could 'hear' everything that was said telepathically.

4. **Intense positive emotions** – feelings of overwhelming love and being loved, peace, compassion, understanding.

5. **Encountering a mystical, brilliant light**.

6. **Meeting other beings** – mystical beings, frequently described as 'beings of light' or deceased relatives or friends. (It is likely that the mystical being or 'light being' is their personal guide. Sometimes a guide may take on the guise of a familiar religious figure because it fulfils expectations, provides comfort and ensures their message gets across.)

7. **A sense of altered time or space** – like regression subjects, people were taken to wherever they thought of being instantly. Also, like regression subjects, NDErs report seeing their past, present and future lives occurring

simultaneously. Some also see alternative or parallel lives. All found it difficult to explain.

8. **Life review** – many NDErs really did see their life flash before their eyes. One subject reported it like a series of slides of moments. All felt that these 'moments' had meaning and generally were related to whether they had behaved lovingly or selfishly. Here is one mentioned in Jeffrey Long's *Evidence of the Afterlife*:

"I began to see my whole life unfolding before me like a film projected on a screen, from babyhood to adult life. It was so real! I was looking at myself, but better than a 3D movie as I was also capable of sensing the feelings of the persons I had interacted with through the years. I could feel the good and bad emotions I made them go through. I was also capable of seeing that the better I made them feel, and the better the emotions they had because of me, [the more] credit [I would accumulate] and that the bad would take some of it back... just like in a bank account, but here it was like a karma account..."

Some were asked if they were ready to die, or if they had achieved what they wanted to achieve. Some were asked what they had done for their fellow man.

Some were told why they needed to go back. Others were told only that they had to go back because there was something they needed to do/ a mission they needed to complete – and that they would know what it was.

9. **Encountering 'heavenly' realms** – like many regression subjects, Brinkley saw 'cathedrals of light' and 'halls of knowledge.' In *Saved by the Light*, he mentions some stories from other NDErs he met. In one, a woman shared that "one of the most interesting things she saw was that prayers were streaming through this heavenly world like rays of light."

10. **Learning special knowledge** – many report an expanded awareness of the reasons and purpose of creation, of the meaning of life, of the universal plan; and learning or being shown the reason why things are the way they are. Dannion Brinkley gives a representative example of this when he writes in *Secrets of the Light,* "I sensed the meticulous perfection and orderly unfolding of the entire universal plan."

Ned Dougherty reports, "I was most affected by my awareness of the energy that permeated all matter. This spiritual energy was a confirmation of God's presence in all levels of existence... I could see the uniqueness of all things, that all particles of existence are directed and controlled by a spiritual energy created by God to regulate the universe."

Most returned from their experience with a new awareness of what is important: "We are all part of the same universe. If we hurt someone else, we hurt ourselves too. It is just that simple." Some NDErs were tasked with letting people know the truth about life – that it doesn't end and that life and love are continuously looking for expression (and not just on Earth).

Brinkley's mission was to establish **spiritualistic capitalism** on Earth. Rather than living in a society ruled by godless capitalism, the beings Brinkley encountered presented the idea of each one of us finding something we love to do and then using that talent or gift to serve the world while also making an income. The beings told him that spiritualistic capitalism was needed because people had to realize that their security is not to be found in governments, institutions, or religions. They need to be shown how to rely on the innate spiritual talents with which each of us have been gifted.

Some, like Dougherty and Brinkley, were shown **visions of the future**. There are 3 categories of these: (1) Some were shown what life would be like for those they would leave behind if they chose to die. Included in this group were those who tried to commit suicide. These unfortunate souls were shown the effect their actions would have on those they loved and were also made aware that they had made a huge mistake in wasting a life. All become aware that they have been given a second chance and are determined to take advantage of it. (2) Some were shown part of their personal future; for example, Mary Neal was told her son would die at 18. This confirmed what her son had known from a young age and already told her! Aware that he had limited time, he achieved some amazing things before he was killed (at age 19) by a driver on his cellphone. (3) Some NDErs were given visions of the future of life on Earth, which will be discussed shortly.

11. **A boundary or barrier that they may not cross**

12. **Return to the physical body** – frequently reluctantly. Some subjects were allowed to choose whether they would come back or not, but most were told it wasn't their time (to die) or that they had something to do. For example, one subject who wanted to stay was told, "You must return; I have given you a task; you have not finished."

These 12 common features of NDEs are paraphrased from *Evidence of the Afterlife (2010)* by Jeffrey Long, M.D., with Paul Perry. (Perry also co-wrote Moody's second book *Life Before Life, 1990,* summarizing Moody's later research into past-life regression.)

The NDErs' out-of-body experience, where the consciousness or personality comes into contact with the afterlife, makes it quite different from the regression experience, during which the conscious mind/ personality is bypassed and direct contact is made with the higher self. In NDEs, it is a spiritual being who provides information about the future; while in future-life progressions, the higher self has direct access to this information. Despite these differences, both experiences provide contact with a source of universal knowledge beyond the physical world.

WHY ARE PEOPLE BEING SHOWN THE FUTURE?

A shift in values

NDEr Dannion Brinkley comments in *At Peace in the Light*, "I find it revealing that people are not coming back from these celestial life reviews with cures for cancer or solutions to our planet's overpopulation. Rather, they are coming back with a message of love, caring and concern for their fellow man. Apparently, this is information that those in the spiritual realm deem pertinent to the human race."

It was probably the effect of the atomic bomb that generated a more universal interest in the future of mankind. You didn't have to be a soothsayer to realize that a third, nuclear, war would have global consequences. There is a common message (and not just from visionaries) that mankind has gotten way off track and needs some serious reminders that we are all in this life together.

Researcher Kevin Williams, provides an extensive list on his page, "The Future and the Near-Death Experience," (see www.near-death.com/science/research/future.html) of reports from NDErs of global catastrophes to come. He notes however, that the goal of an apocalyptic prophecy is not to frighten people – or even to prove the prophet correct – but to warn people to change in order to prevent what has been prophesized from happening.

"The flow of human events can be changed, but first people have to know what they are." – Dannion Brinkley.

CATASTROPHE AND SPIRITUAL AWAKENING LINKED

A famous prophecy

A 1934 prophecy that concerned many due to the accuracy of Cayce's pronouncements and his apparent access to a 'higher' source of information, which he called the Akashic Records, was the following:

"The earth will be broken up in the western portion of America. The greater portion of Japan must go into the sea. The upper portion of Europe will be changed as in the twinkling of an eye. Land will appear off the east coast of America. There will be the upheavals in the Arctic and in the Antarctic that will make for the eruption of volcanoes in the torrid areas, and there will be the shifting then of the poles – so that where there have been those of a frigid or semitropical will become the more tropical, and moss and fern will grow. And these will begin in those periods in '58 to '98 when these will be proclaimed as the periods when His Light will be seen again in the clouds."

Many researchers were interested in the validity of this prediction because of its dire implications for the planet, including well-known past-life researcher, Helen Wambach, whose subjects seemed to confirm the Cayce prophecy. Under hypnotic progression, they too saw increasingly severe climate problems leading to a major catastrophe (earthquake and flooding of landmasses, in particular through the middle of America) sometime in the late nineties. Clearly, and fortunately, this did not happen – or hasn't happened yet.

Some, in particular NDE researcher Kevin Williams, suggest that as Cayce's prophecies became well-known all over the world, they influenced enough people to create sociological change and alter the course of history. Others suggest that Cayce's prediction will still happen; he just got the timing wrong.

Cayce remarked that even the Lord of Lords (Jesus, Revelations) could not accurately predict future events because human free will can alter and change the future!

Spiritual awakening: en-light-enment

In 1938, Cayce predicted, "A new order of conditions is to arise" and, ultimately, a new era of enlightenment and peace. Fifty years later, many NDErs were coming back with the same message: mankind would evolve and live in universal harmony – but only after a period of catastrophic natural disasters. Their accounts of the future visions they were shown seem to imply that global upheaval was an inevitable part of this process. Cayce, however, repeatedly commented that a return to spiritual/ enlightened values could avert the worst of these disasters.

He said "...there must be a purging in high places as well as low; and that there must be the greater consideration of the individual, so that each soul being his brother's keeper;" otherwise, "a leveling will occur."

Catastrophe is the great leveler – in more ways than one. It was the catastrophes of two world wars and the atrocities of Nazism that led to the founding of the United Nations in 1945 and, in 1948, the Universal Declaration of Human Rights: *"All human beings are born free and equal in dignity and rights. They are endowed with reason and conscience and should act towards one another in the spirit of brotherhood."* Its 30 articles make inspiring reading. The Declaration of Human Rights became universal law in 1976 – although in 1990 Muslim countries chose to adopt a version based on Islam (in which religious freedom is limited and women do not have equal rights with men).

There is no doubt that major sociological changes occurred in the period '58-'98: among other things, the New Age Movement – people becoming more aware of their spiritual nature and essential unity; the end of apartheid; the fall of the iron curtain. Could it be that "His Light" was appearing in the clouds of human consciousness?

Sources as diverse as Dolores Cannon (*The Three Waves of Volunteers and the New Earth*) and NDEr Mellen-Thomas Benedict observe that the 'second coming of the Christ' does not mean the return of a person, but an awakening of spiritual consciousness – which both agree is already underway.

Ian Lawton is a British researcher of ancient civilizations and spiritual philosophy. In *Book of the Soul (2008)*, he observes that, in their original form, Mayan calendrical predictions focused on the year 2012 seem to be at least as much about spiritual awakening as they are about any form of catastrophe. He observes: "Perhaps we are ready for a major spiritual awakening, which does need a major catastrophe to precipitate it and to strip out all the deadwood of materialism. Or perhaps by choosing a more spiritual path of our own volition humanity can avoid the need for such a catastrophe."

This 'spiritual path' can take many forms as the following examples from regression subjects and NDErs show.

ALTERNATIVE FUTURES

Just as there are alternative futures to choose from in the Bardo (between lives), our choices in this present life will determine which of at least two future lives we will inhabit. It is possible that there are infinite possible futures for us all – and that these interconnect in a way that only theoretical physicists and God can understand! The 1998 movie *Sliding Doors*, starring Gwyneth Paltrow and John Hannah, is an entertaining depiction of this concept.

Both FLP therapists, Brian Weiss and Anne Jirsch have found clear evidence of alternative futures; Weiss, in particular, that a change of values in this lifetime can result in completely a different future.

In Same Soul, Many Bodies – Discover the healing power of future lives through progression therapy (2004), Dr. Weiss describes a Jewish client, Evelyn, who came to him filled with despondency and rage over the situation in the Middle East. Her frustration was also ruining her marriage, as her Jewish husband wasn't angry about the situation and she felt he should be. Dr. Weiss tried conventional psychotherapy, exploring her background and childhood, but the causes of her anger and despondency didn't seem to reside there. He suggested a regression and she agreed.

Evelyn discovered she had been a Nazi officer in a former life, a member of the SS supervising the loading of Jews into cattle cars. They were vermin and he hated having to waste bullets on the ones he shot trying to escape! This didn't surprise Dr. Weiss. Evelyn's pro-Israel stance in this life was a compensation for her anti-Semitism in her previous one. Weiss reports that he has discovered that the surest way to be reincarnated into a particular group of people, defined by religion, race, nationality or culture, is to hate those people in a previous life. Evelyn's hatred for Jews in her previous life had now been transformed into an equal hatred for Arabs.

What to do?

As Dr. Weiss explained to Evelyn, he believes we are able to influence our future lives by what we do in this one. Stands to reason! He asked her if she'd like to progress to her next probable lifetime to see what would happen if she stays on her present course of hatred and rage. She agreed. It will be no surprise to anybody to discover that in her next life she is a poor Muslim girl, living in the Palestinian territories, angry at the rich Jews who are perpetuating the war. In a life after that, she is a Christian man living in Africa, angry at the rapidly growing Hindu population in his part of the world.

When Evelyn reviewed her lives, she realized that there would always be people to hate and blame, but then she had an epiphany – violence only perpetuates the suffering; compassion and love are the antidotes to hatred and rage. (Didn't Gandhi... and the Dalai Lama...? Sometimes you have to live it to learn it!)

The next step in Dr. Weiss's treatment is even more interesting. He asked Evelyn to progress to a future life which would eventuate if she is able to let go of all of her current prejudices and anger. She finds that her future life changes completely. She is the manager of a hotel and spa in Hawaii. Guests arrive from all over the world – different countries and cultures mingle happily.

As Weiss points out, there is no way of validating future-life progressions. However, if a future-life progression, authentic or not, gives a client insight into her life and behavior, then it works! Nevertheless, his findings confirm Cayce's statement, made 60 years earlier: "We prepare for future lifetimes during the life we live now."

Weiss reports that Evelyn decided to change her life both outwardly – she found a new job that gave her back her joi de vivre – and inwardly; she let go of her anger. By experiencing the lives of the people she hated, she understood that to hate them is to hate ourselves.

NOT SET IN STONE

While Weiss had his clients experience two possible futures, FLP therapist Anne Jirsch believes that we have four possible future paths to choose from at moments of crucial decisions – ranging from best potential outcome to least favorable. Extrapolating from this, it is possible that our global future too could follow at least four potential paths. Wambach's subjects, in *Mass Dreams of the Future,* foresaw four distinct types of future (see 17. Future Lifestyles).

Every NDEr who came back with a message/ warning about the future similarly emphasized that the future is not fixed. All were told that the future is changing from moment to moment based upon our current (individual) actions and decisions – and where we place our attention. Cayce and Nostradamus reiterated this message.

Nostradamus referred to alternative futures as timelines. He explained to Dolores that in the course of world events, there are 'nexus points' – events of major impact; and from them, effects branch out to create a number of possible future timelines, from the best to the worst, thus the future is not one preset path. He also believed that the timelines he foresaw might possibly be turned to more positive outcomes if enough people heeded his warnings.

Nostradamus found it hard to predict the exact timing of events, but told Cannon that if he knew the position of the constellations in the sky in her time he could give an indication. Dolores knew nothing about constellations, but a week later she met John, an astrologer, who became her next subject, through whom she again made contact with Nostradamus.

Upon regression, Dolores discovered that in his life just past, John had been an astrologer for Hitler. He was one of a group of astrologists asked by Hitler to corrupt Nostradamus's quatrains to prove that Germany would win the war. These corrupted messages were then printed on pamphlets and dropped over countries in Europe. John was shot in that life for refusing to continue with his task once he realized what was happening to the Jews. (His wife in the Nazi lifetime brought home a new lampshade and John was sickened to discover it was made of human skin from Dachau.) In this life he was fulfilling a karmic debt by helping to accurately translate the quatrains.

During the nineties, Dolores travelled all over the world talking and lecturing to metaphysical groups and others. She felt that she had achieved her mission as many of the things Nostradamus predicted have not happened. The world is on a different timeline from the one he foresaw.

A PARADIGM CHALLENGE

A tricky thing about looking into the future is that we do it from the paradigm we know. For example, a famous 17th century prophecy of the Brahan Seer of Scotland was, "The day will come when long strings of carriages without horses shall run between Dingwall and Inverness." He was describing the coming of the railway in the 19th century. Imagine trying to explain Facebook, sexting and segways to the people of those days!

In addition, some of the developments we may look for from the future, e.g. increased longevity or a cure for cancer, may have no meaning in a future time, as sources see the physical structure of the body evolving to become less and less dense, with the consciousness able to leave the body at will. As Anita Moorjani found in *Dying to be Me,* the cure for her cancer was not the answer to her problem. When she didn't heal her spirit by following her own goals, the cancer returned. As mankind progresses, values will change; and as history has repeatedly shown, things we now accept as fact – and limitation – will be proven not to be so.

The good news is that in 1000 years, it will all be peachy, but unsurprisingly it will not be "life as we know it." Understanding visions of our future selves in terms of the current parameters of what is possible and what isn't may be a challenge!

The bad news is that Nostradamus isn't the only one who foresaw "dark times" along the way. Descriptions of possible futures follow.

COMMON VISIONS OF THE FUTURE

1. A crucial time in Earth's history

A number of the NDEs that featured catastrophic visions of the future occurred in the 1980s which suggests that this was a crucial time for humanity. Certainly, a lot more messages from the other side began to emerge in one form or another. While many prophecies came true, a significant number did not or did not occur in such a drastic form as originally foretold.

Both Edgar Cayce and NDErs shown prophetic visions reported that if humanity changed its values, then the future would change and these visions would not occur. It was made clear that our common future changes with every *individual* decision. For example, during Karen Schaeffer's NDE following a car accident, she was shown her children's future as it would exist if she decided to remain in the light. Because she decided to return, the future she was shown did not happen.

According to the light beings that Howard Storm encountered, "God wishes to usher in a new 'kingdom' within the next 200 years. In order to do so, God has rescinded some of the free will he had given to his creatures in favor of more divine control over the world." Dougherty makes similar comments and suggests that this is why we are getting more interactions with beings from the afterlife. He believes that the years leading up to 2034 (i.e. the 50 years following his NDE) will be a critical period for humanity.

Clearly some world prognostications, e.g. WW3 and the poles shifting, have not eventuated within the timeframe given. Some say they may yet happen. Many prophecies concern America, but they might point the way for all of us.

As recently as 2000, NDEr Lance Richardson (*The Message*), son of Idaho's state senator, was told during his encounter with two guides/ friends in the afterlife, one of whom had been a founding father of America, to write a book recounting his NDE: "That this message may prick the hearts of many, help awaken them to the awful condition to which your country has declined, remind them of the multitude of prophecies which have been given concerning your day, and open their eyes to the fact that these same prophecies are being fulfilled before their eyes."

The answer, Richardson was told, is service. "It is the mode of heaven. Each seeks for the betterment of the whole, not themselves... And if you will serve one another, your nation will be transformed into a haven of real peace and freedom."

Unlike Richardson, the earlier NDErs and Cayce and Nostradamus, later accounts of NDEs (e.g. *To Heaven and Back* by Dr Mary Neal, *Dying to Be Me* by Anita Moorjani, and *Proof of Heaven* by Dr Eben Alexander, all published in 2012) don't seem to contain such dire messages for the future, or indeed any world prophecies. This may indicate that humanity is on an improved timeline.

Further evidence is given by FLP therapist Anne Jirsch and her subjects/ participants, who don't report any sign of catastrophe within the next 100 years. Dr. Brian Weiss's clients don't foresee anything cataclysmic for at least 300 years. However, that's not to say we're out of the woods!

2. No nuclear war/ WW3

Nostradamus predicted WW3 starting at the end of the 1990s resulting from the actions of a man he called the Antichrist – a humanitarian turned corrupt with power. (Fortunately, no figure like this has emerged.) Nostradamus believed this war would involve nuclear weapons, so he told Dolores to publish her books to tell people to use the power of their minds to prevent it from happening.

Like other future-time visionaries, Nostradamus observed that the future is malleable. Individuals have the power to change the future. One decision can change an entire timeline. However, he also emphasized the power of the 'group mind' – that groups of like-minded people praying for peace were many times more powerful than individuals.

Howard Storm's NDE, in 1985, was when the world was in the grip of the Cold War between Communism and Democracy. With both the U.S. and Russia, and probably China, stockpiling nuclear arms, nuclear war and its consequent planet-wide destruction was a distinct possibility. However, Storm was told that the Cold War would soon end, which it did, because "God is changing the hearts of people to love around the world." He was also told, definitely, that there would be no nuclear war. Thus WW3, the nuclear war predicted by Cayce and shown to some NDErs (with the proviso as happening *unless mankind changes its behavior*), now seems unlikely.

Dannion Brinkley was shown the Chernobyl disaster (which happened in 1986, 11 years after his NDE) and a later nuclear disaster in a badly polluted northern sea, which did not. He was also shown people losing faith in the government of the Soviet Union as a result of these disasters, its subsequent collapse and a time of struggle, all of which occurred.

Howard Storm asked the question that many of us have asked: Why are wars allowed? The light-beings Storm encountered, who he refers to as his friends, (who showed him his life review and were most likely his 'council of elders' – advanced beings above the level of guides – see *Past Life Lessons*) replied that out of all the wars humanity had tried to start, they allowed a few to bring people to their senses in order to prevent future ones.

Another startling revelation was given to NDEr, Mellen-Thomas Benedict. Before his NDE in 1982, Benedict had many post-WW2 concerns: toxic waste, nuclear missiles, the population explosion, erosion of the rainforests. During his NDE he was told that the nuclear mushroom cloud, *as a symbol*, has done more than any religion or philosophy on Earth to bring mankind together, to a new level of consciousness that says "Enough," and to the recognition that accumulating more bombs to make sure that no one wins a nuclear war is not the answer to man's survival.

3. Natural disasters and climate changes

Many NDErs, (Dannion Brinkley, Dr. George Ritchie, Ned Dougherty and others not mentioned here but who can be found on Kevin Williams' website) as well as both Edgar Cayce and Nostradamus, prophesized catastrophic natural disasters in the form of earthquakes, volcanic eruptions, tidal waves, and unusual or devastating climatic events like hurricanes and tornadoes, droughts and flooding. All of these have been a major feature of the 21st century to date.

Past-life therapist Glenn Williston, *Discovering Your Past Lives (1983),* mentions a client who spontaneously jumped ahead to a future life in San Francisco following the rebuilding of the city. It had been destroyed by a devastating earthquake. The year is 2085.

Some future visionaries saw a dramatic rise in ocean levels and a shift in the Earth's axis, resulting in warm weather where there used to be cold and vice versa. Those who saw the rise in the oceans also predicted land sinking into the sea or being covered by water, most notably parts of the eastern coast of America, parts of Middle America and the east coast of Japan.

Edgar Cayce's 1934 prophecy, "The greater portion of Japan must go into the sea," has since been associated with the magnitude 9 earthquake that struck off the east coast of Japan in 2011 resulting in a tsunami that covered 400 km (250 miles) of coastline and travelled up to 10 km (6 miles) inland. Geophysicists estimate that the quake shifted the island of Honshu 2.4 meters (8 feet) and the Earth on its axis between

10 and 25 cm (4-10 inches). In addition, 400 km of the northeast coast of Japan dropped vertically 0.6 meters (2 feet).

Dolores Cannon's clients also report earth changes to come. The signs of upcoming changes are given: first, there would be quakes where they've always occurred; then quakes where there have never been. Second, watch the Ring of Fire – volcanoes awakening. Third, weather will become increasingly strange, cold areas that would become hot and vice versa, drought – "a year without a rainbow," then rain.

For those who wonder what to do, both Cannon and future-life researcher Chet Snow advise following your instincts about where to go to be safe (not California or Florida). Snow adds, "Keep away from water."

Connection between 'acts of God' and acts of man
NDE researcher Margot Grey was told by one of her subjects that current catastrophic Earth changes are a reflection of the social upheaval and violence that is happening all over the world at the moment. The recognition of this causal connection between man and nature is not new.

Paramahansa Yogananda (1893-1952), an Indian yogi who brought Eastern philosophy to America and founded the worldwide Self Realization Fellowship Movement, said: "The sudden cataclysms that occur in nature... are not 'acts of God.' Such disasters result from the thoughts and actions of man. Whenever the world's vibratory balance of good and evil is disturbed by an accumulation of harmful vibrations, the result of man's wrong thinking and wrong doing, you will see devastation..."

And similarly, "Wars are bought about not by fateful divine action, but by widespread material selfishness... When materiality predominates in man's consciousness, there is an emission of subtle negative rays [vibrations]; their cumulative

41

power disturbs the electrical balance of nature, and that is when earthquakes, floods and other disasters happen."

Japanese scientist, Dr. Masaru Emoto agrees. Since the mid-90s, he has done extensive research with water crystals demonstrating the positive and negative influence of human words and thoughts on matter. He states in *Hidden Messages in Water (2004)* that his research has led him to conclude: "The waters of the world are reacting to human energy patterns, causing many of these disasters." Cayce also stated in his readings that sunspots, which affect many of our communications systems, are caused more by human attitudes and emotions than cosmic forces.

NDEr Rainee Pasarow had it explained like this: "There will be tremendous upheaval in the world as a result of humanity's general ignorance of true reality... Humanity is being consumed by the cancers of arrogance, materialism, racism, chauvinism and separatist thinking... Humanity is breaking the laws of the universe, and as a result of this, humanity will suffer. This suffering will not be due to the wrath of God, but rather like the pain one might suffer by arrogantly defying the law of gravity."

Thus it appears that the natural disasters we are currently experiencing are the *accumulated* consequences of breaking these universal laws. Falling on the just and the unjust, earthquakes, hurricanes and flooding are occurring at times and distances separate from the events that generated them. They are a devastating reminder that the Earth is a closed system.

In the future, however, there is recognition amongst the more enlightened of the negative energy causing natural disasters, and people around the world unite in prayer to ameliorate it. (See 9. Greater awareness of the power of prayer.)

4. Worldwide food shortage

A number of NDErs were shown people fighting each other over food, poverty and starvation. Different causes are given: the collapse of the economy in America, dramatic climatic events, catastrophic geophysical disaster. Howard Storm was shown disruption of food supplies in America; Ricky Randolph saw Americans killing for food and water; Margot Grey that: "There are going to be serious food shortages around the world due to droughts in many places. This will push the price of food up so that many people will have to start going without things they have always taken for granted."

Ned Dougherty was told world events would alter the availability and distribution of food supplies, and worldwide hunger would become a massive problem. Despite the fact that many men, women and children were dying of starvation, there was still enough food in the world to feed everyone. However, the avarice of those in control prevented it from being adequately distributed.

5. Shifting of the poles

Both Edgar Cayce and Nostradamus predict a pole shift, with many areas that are now land again becoming ocean floor, and land (Atlantis) rising off the coast of Florida (Bimini).

According to Nostradamus, 'earth jarrings' are forewarnings of an Earth Shift – a minor tilt of the Earth's axis – cause unknown but possibly, he suggested, due to a nuclear war that disrupts the Earth's magnetic field or possibly from the effect of a previously unknown comet that he says will herald the Earth Changes. People will perish from huge tidal waves and fires sweeping through cities. (Evidently this is the grim message of Revelation 16.) He has even worked out the exact date – 24 October 2029.

Some will not be prepared as they will refuse to heed advice from non-scientific sources. Nostradamus noted that the world would only have to tilt just a fraction for the continents to start shifting and places to flood. There would be huge upheavals as the tectonic plates would push against each other and force some low-lying parts upwards.

Nostradamus gives the surviving population as 120 million. There will be worldwide weather changes; for example, hail storms will destroy the food-producing areas of America, Russia, England and Australia. There will be worldwide famine and disease.

Nostradamus foresaw much of the world covered by water – with land comprising only about 10% of the globe; (it is presently about 30%). In addition, the U.S., much of Europe and the African continent become groups of islands, and only the long narrow mountainous region of South America will remain. The Alps in Europe will form the new shoreline while most of France and the Low Countries will be under water. India will be under water up to the foothills of the Himalayas.

Only the mountains of England and Scotland will remain (as islands). Hawaii and Alaska are submerged, as are the Philippines, most of SE Asia, the Arabian peninsula and Italy. Japan's islands would be smaller but would eventually grow from its active volcanoes.

Iceland will be larger. New continents in the Atlantic and Pacific emerge from the ocean floor. The interior of Russia and China remain, but much of China would be islands created from the mountain tops. There would be a large shallow inland sea which could eventually be drained to reclaim the land.

Australia is one of the 'lucky' continents – not much changed although it will suffer damage from great storms sweeping the Earth and, since the poles have shifted, will have a new location. The inhabitants will not be quite so lucky, as coastal cities endure tidal waves and the central desert fierce storms and flash floods. Following these climatic upheavals, however, the climate will be more moderate everywhere.

Maps of the future shape of world as seen by Nostradamus are given in *Conversations with Nostradamus, Vol. 3.* The polar ice caps are gone and will not reform for several hundred years.

To alleviate the effects of this disaster
Nostradamus advises that people should continue with new technology and space programs. There is the possibility that solar-powered space stations will be developed before the shift occurs. These could beam down energy which could speed up the rebuilding process (because a primary problem will be loss of electricity to power communications and machinery). Nostradamus also predicts that it will take only 10-15 years for technology be back to the level it was before the shift.

An alternative timeline
Nostradamus believed "forewarned is forearmed" and that by showing Dolores the worst possible scenario, it may be that present-day man will do something to prevent it. In her video lecture on YouTube, 2012, Dolores felt this to be the case as, after translating the 1000 quatrains and being encouraged by Nostradamus to travel all over the world and spread this message, her communications with him ceased. A hopeful indication that we are on an alternative timeline from the one that Nostradamus foresaw is that he told Dolores that the Earth Shift would be in her lifetime; however, she died in 2014.

Brian Weiss confirms that we seem to have avoided the worst – for now at least. The participants of his study report a world that is pretty much unchanged going into the next century: more toxins, more crowding, more pollution and more global warming, but fewer diseases and better methods for growing and harvesting food; calamities as usual, but nothing global. His individual cases, however, suggest there are places on Earth where there has been a shift in consciousness.

6. Melting of the ice-caps

Many sources predict major changes to the surface of the Earth through flooding. Participants of FLP researcher Anne Jirsch report that by 2100 the oceans will have risen worldwide as the icecaps melt, submerging coastal promenades and piers. Much of the American coastline will recede with New Orleans vanishing. Florida will be flooded.

In 1936, Edgar Cayce reported a similar outcome. He foresaw his next reincarnation in a greatly changed U.S.A.

"I had been born again in 2100 A.D. in Nebraska. The sea apparently covered all of the western part of the country, as the city where I lived was on the coast. The family name was a strange one. At an early age as a child I declared myself to be Edgar Cayce who had lived 200 years before. Scientists, men with long beards, little hair and thick glasses, were called in to observe me. They decided to visit the places where I said I had been born, lived and worked in Kentucky, Alabama, New York, Michigan and Virginia.

Taking me with them the group of scientists visited these places in a long, cigar-shaped metal flying ship which moved at a high speed. Water covered part of Alabama. Norfolk, Virginia, had become an immense seaport. New York had been destroyed either by war or an immense earthquake and was being rebuilt. Industries were scattered over the countryside. Most of the houses were built of glass. Many records of my work as Edgar Cayce were discovered and collected. The group returned to Nebraska, taking the records with them to study..."

7. A reduced population

One thing that almost all of the future visions reveal is a greatly reduced human population. This is confirmed by another source, Bruce Moen, (*Voyages into the Afterlife, 1999*). Moen was told the following information when he asked about the 'Big Plan for the Earth' in the near future.

Overconsumption

"In general the Earth's near future is preparation for large population reductions. This will reduce human impact on the ecosystem. The primary cause is indulgence in the emotional energy of greed. Consumption of Earth's resources has been accelerating, primarily not for direct use, but rather for accumulation of wealth. That coupled with an extremely large human population is pushing the ecosystem toward collapse." Moen was also told that many on Earth are working to mitigate the ecosystem situation. Two things that remain unclear regarding this drastic population decrease, however, are when and how.

Dr. Chet Snow's continued investigations into the mass consciousness led him to the prophecies and visions of indigenous cultures like Arizona's Hopi nation and the Australian Aborigines. He discovered that these indigenous seers too foretell a massive decline in world population but do not identify a reason.

Pollution

A number of FLP subjects report that pollution of the air, water and soil has resulted in greatly reduced fertility in all living species, including man. As I write this in August 2017, an international study of men in first world countries has revealed that in the last 20 years, fertility has decreased by 50%. No single cause has been identified.

In a recent interview with world-famous naturalist David Attenborough, he was asked to describe the biggest change he has seen in over half a century of studying animal life on the planet. He replied that the population of humanity had trebled in that time. He had just watched an albatross coming back from its search across the oceans for food for its young. As it opened its beak for its fledglings clamouring with hunger, Sir David saw that it was filled with discarded plastic it had scooped up from the ocean surface, which it thought was food.

In *Journey of Souls (1994)*, past-life regression therapist and researcher Michael Newton mentions that some of his subjects were able to see "snatches of the future" in the Bardo during their planning for their next life. "[S]some have told me earth's population will be greatly reduced by the end of the twenty-second century [2199], partially due to adverse soil and atmospheric changes. They also see people living in odd-looking domed buildings." (In the Wambach/ Snow study, participants also mention domed buildings. See Lifestyles further on.)

Weapons research
Nostradamus described biological weapons causing plagues, disruption of food supplies and starvation; a mistake in weapons research that ruptures protective fields surrounding Earth, so that the Earth actually attracts meteors and other space debris (some have connected this to the HAARP project in Alaska which shoots high frequency waves into the ionosphere to study its effect on communications); and weapons that alter the weather patterns on the planet that also cause major outbreaks of birth defects. Hopefully, a timeline involving secret weapons research, and its consequences, has been averted.

Global calamity
Brian Weiss's clients also predict a dark time ahead. In 300-600 years (2300-2600) there will begin a second Dark Ages. This time seems to be advancing more quickly because of the negative thoughts and actions of many people. He comments that it is not just those who think violence is the way to solve injustices, but because too many of us are selfish, materialistic and lacking in empathy and compassion. Our urge to do good is subsumed by our desire to be physically comfortable. He also notes that there is a vastly diminished population at this time, possibly due to some sort of global calamity.

John, a client of Dr. Weiss, gives us his view of this future time. John is an extremely wealthy man with no particular religious or spiritual inclinations. His visit to Dr. Weiss is due to an increasingly debilitating fear of death. His current life seems to have no causal relation to his fears, so he was taken back through his past lives.

Unfortunately for John, these showed a pattern of power and selfishness, with rape, murder and other unpleasantness thrown in; lives in which he had ignored opportunities to display compassion. Dr. Weiss then takes him to a future life. In a hypnotic trance, John finds himself with two spiritual guides who lead him to a fork in the road that indicates the way to future lifetimes.

First they take him to the future life he would experience if he continues on with his present hedonistic lifestyle unchanged. He sees himself as an unhappily married American woman collecting her baby from a laboratory. The baby is part of an advanced cloning procedure which had been perfected as human fertility and birth rates plummet due to chemical toxins in food, water and air. Technology accidents have made many areas uninhabitable. Farms and forests have disappeared and people live in huge city-states that are often at war with each other. Science and technology have advanced, as often for ill as for good, but human ambition and prejudices have not changed. Synthetic foods have helped allay hunger, but pollution threatens fish and the water supply.

After visiting this route, John is taken along the future route he would follow if he chooses a more compassionate, charitable and generous approach in his current life. This time he sees himself as the president of a prestigious university in what had been America before all national boundaries disappeared. He's rich and happily married, using his money for scholarships to attract talented students to his university. They and his faculty all look for ways to create unity among people by encouraging an emphasis on similarities, not differences, between them. He is renowned, but that means nothing compared to the joy he gets from life.

As you can guess, John made changes, He began to channel his immense wealth into projects that benefitted the community and, although he had no material need to work or study, took courses in economics and management so he could take over the running of his charities. His fear of death evaporated in his newfound lease on a life of 'doing good.'

(Does anybody else notice shades of Charles Dickens' A Christmas Carol, written in 1843, with Ebenezer Scrooge and his ghosts of Christmases past, present and yet to come?)

8.   Greater value placed on the environment

According to the participants of Jirsch's study, by 2025, many cities in Europe, the U.K., America, China and the Far East will have a problem with pollution. Norway, however, will lead the way with clean efficient travel and a breakthrough in handling pollution, winning a Nobel Prize in a new category: Services to the Planet.

Recycling becomes a major political issue along with less packaging. One company will become very successful producing biodegradable packaging that will enrich the soil. Many more people will grow their own fruit and vegetables.

NDEr Mellen-Thomas Benedict was told "the clearing of the rainforest will slow down, and in fifty years [i.e. by 2032] there will be more trees on the planet than in a long time... Earth is in the process of domesticating itself. It is never again going to be as wild a place as it once was. There will be great wild places, reserves where nature thrives. Gardening and reserves will be the thing in the future."

Jirsch sees a different picture. By 2100, forest areas have declined so are now protected. The climate of England is more tropical. People have adapted to continuing global warming. Parts of the Middle East as well as Africa have become barren and uninhabitable. With an increasing world population, water will become more precious all over the globe. Scientists will have some success with weather control to supply water to drought-stricken areas. Scientists have also developed particles that, released into the air, 'eat up' pollutants.

Earlier widespread use of nuclear power has transitioned into solar and wind power – and possibly other new sources. Many homes have their own generator and recycle their water. There is also a form of natural fuel that is grown, renewable and creates a lot of energy with low CO_2 emissions.

Environmentalism – the new religion
Many NDErs similarly foresee a new respect for the environment. After awful images of nuclear disaster and pollution, Brinkley "understood that environmentalism would emerge as the world's new religion. People would consider a clean environment a key to salvation more than they ever had before. Political parties would spring up around the issue of a cleaner planet and political fortunes would be made or broken based upon feelings about the environment."

On a *seemingly* unrelated topic, Cayce foretold: "On Russia's religious development will come the greater hope of the world."

Thirty years after Brinkley's first NDE, the early years of the new millennium saw an amazing series of books come out of Russia, inspiring huge ideological and sociological changes, not just in Russia but creating a worldwide movement. Called *The Ringing Cedars* series by Vladimir Megre, they tell a story of the meeting of a Russian trader (the author of the books) with elders of a remote village deep in the forests of Siberia.

The series is based upon the wisdom of Anastasia, the daughter of one of the elders, a survivor of an ancient Vedic civilization whose extraordinary powers and knowledge far exceed anything known today. Anastasia's messages about living in tune with nature and educating children to bring out their inner wisdom offer a whole new paradigm for our planet's future that is already being followed by groups all over the world. (This ideal is very similar to the vision of the ideal future given to Howard Storm during his NDE. See Postscript.)

Nostradamus also foresees a movement "back to the earth," when people will be tearing down cities to have more land to farm; not because there is a desperate need for food, but because of the profound shift in values after troubled times.

This seems to be the path of at least one future timeline for the Earth. *Dr. Weiss's client, Christina, progressed just over a thousand years to the date 3200, reports that the earth is very green, much more fertile than now; the forests are lush, but even though there is plenty of food available, there are no animals. There are fewer people and they live in small groups, not cities, in houses made of wood or stone. They seem to be farmers. Liquid light pours into the plants and people, connecting everyone and everything in peace.*

9. Greater awareness of the power of prayer

On this topic, FLP therapist Brian Weiss gives the example of David, a WASP (White, Anglo-Saxon Protestant) from New England, who'd had some pretty interesting past lives and 'done good' in most of them. David was progressed to 100 years into the future and saw himself as a rabbi at a conference with ministers and healers of all denominations. They meet 2-3 times a week to meditate and pray, creating a harmonious energy to combat the hate and violence of the unenlightened. Their purpose is to neutralize the Earth-damaging energies unknowingly unleashed by those who don't know or care about spiritual laws. Those energies create earthquakes, tornadoes, floods and epidemics, which used to be considered random events, but in this (future) time are believed to be generated or at least influenced by the thoughts and intentions of humankind. They are now preventable!

This group has thousands of followers who carry their teachings back to their own countries – Catholic, Protestant, Hindu, Buddhist, Muslim – all across the globe. Thanks to their efforts the Earth is now cooling for the first time in centuries, weather is less severe and cancer rates are down.

David has also learned how to teach others the way to invoke beings of higher consciousness. "By seeking a higher spiritual good we can seek aid from them. They have already begun to help. The world is a far, far better place than it was 100 years ago."

For readers who find the whole idea of thoughts influencing nature incredible, Japanese scientist, Dr. Masaru Emoto (*The Hidden Messages in Water* and *The Secret Life of Water*) describes an occasion at Fujiwara Dam in central Japan, when a Shinto priest performed an incantation (spoken prayer) over the cloudy lake water for about an hour. Dr. Emoto took samples of the water before and after. About 15 minutes after the prayer, Dr. Emoto's video crew noticed that the water in the lake was becoming increasingly more transparent as they watched until they were eventually able to see even the waterplants at the bottom of the lake.

In a similar experiment, in September 1999, Dr. Emoto invited 350 people to the banks of Lake Biwa, Japan's largest lake, in an attempt to clean the lake through the power of words! Another purpose of the gathering was to pray for peace as the world entered a new century. The crowd joined forces in an affirmation of peace that could be heard around the lake. A month after this event the newspapers reported that the putrid algae that usually appeared each year, and caused an unbearable stench, was absent that year.

Dr. Emoto and his supporters have since prayed for water in Lake Lucerne and Lake Zurich in Switzerland, water in the Bahamas, water in Uchi Lake, Oklahoma, and tap water in Japan, none of which was of a quality to form crystals beforehand. Before and after pictures clearly show the difference made by prayer in revitalizing water, as shown by the resultant creation of ice crystal structures that resemble those of natural spring and river water.

Dr. Emoto concludes that the lesson we can learn from these experiments is that the vibration of good words has a positive effect on our world and the vibration from negative words has the power to destroy. Dr. Emoto sees water as a metaphor for the human soul. Water has become polluted in the same way our collective soul has become polluted with negative emotions like greed, anxiety, anger and despair.

10. Children – a new perspective

A number of NDErs were shown their future children. Dougherty was shown the children he would have had, had he led a less self-centered life, as well as a future child. At the conclusion of his book, *Fast Lane to Heaven,* Dougherty says:

"The most important lesson that I learned on the Other Side is the importance of bringing children into the world. They are our spiritual brothers and sisters who are waiting in God's world to be born into the realm of this world. It is our relationship with our children and our experiences with them that give us our closest connection to God."

NDEr Betty Eadie and others met the adult selves of their future children in the afterlife and understood that there was a covenant between them to be part of each other's mission in life.

Howard Storm foresaw that children would be valued beyond everything. In the vision of the future he was shown, "all [people] participated in child-rearing and teaching as the most important activity of their lives." People in the future will spend most of their time raising children and teaching them to live in harmony with nature.

11. Contact with extra-terrestrials

Almost all of the sources I have included: Cayce, Nostradamus, Weiss, Jirsch, Cannon and a number of NDErs have said that intergalactic contact will happen and it will be a good thing. However, there is no common agreement on *when* this will happen.

Weiss, Jirsch and Wambach do not see it happening until at least 2250. However, Nostradamus sees it happening much earlier, after the Earth Shift in the 21st century. He tells Cannon that there will be visitations by the 'Watchers,' extraterrestrials who keep an eye on humankind's development – as events happening here on Earth could have cosmic consequences. There are records of UFO sightings since biblical times. Perhaps it is not a coincidence that a wave of UFO sightings over the theatres of WW2 began in the 1940s – from whence came the term 'flying saucers' – and has continued thereafter.

Cannon comments that watching the course of events/ destruction on Earth will have spiritual lessons for other more evolved beings, and adds that there will also be spiritual guardians of the Earth helping. Michael Newton (*Destiny of Souls, 2004*) also mentions 'Watchers,' but they are spiritual guardians rather than extra-terrestrials.

To add to the mystery, Bruce Moen, mentioned earlier, also came into contact with alien observers in his *Voyages into the Afterlife.* They were present to learn from the spiritual progress mankind was making during the Earth Changes. (The 'Earth Changes' referred to by Moen seem to refer to both physical and spiritual changes.) The ETs communicated telepathically and operated on a different vibrational level from that visible to earthly consciousness. They told Moen they were members of a galactic federation which Earth would join after the changes.

Both Nostradamus and Wambach report extra-terrestrials, with their superior technology, coming to our aid after the pole shift. In particular, our galactic neighbors will help with technological advancements to explore and colonize space. This will be necessary as, in the not too distant future, not much land mass is left on Earth.

Some of my other references report ongoing contact with extraterrestrials right from the 'seeding' of the earth until now (most notably Dolores Cannon, *The Convoluted Universe* series and *The Custodians*). In her book, *The Three Waves of Volunteers,* she notes that according to her clients, the purpose of alien abductions is to assess the extent of pollutants in human bodies and also to extract DNA – for seeding future hybrid races elsewhere in the universe or perhaps other dimensions. (As well as comments in her works that the human race is some sort of galactic evolutionary experiment, this monitoring and genetic retrieval is strongly analogous to the way we here on Earth treat protected species!)

12. Space travel

In FLP therapist Anne Jirsch's very first case of a client spontaneously jumping ahead to a future life, the puzzled client sees herself as captain of a spacecraft in 2050. A later client similarly sees herself aboard a spacecraft, in uniform, and tells Jirsch this is where they live. In her future visions study, participants report that over the next few decades America will lead a new space race and find evidence of life on Mars. In addition, a new space station will monitor earthquakes, volcanic eruptions, nuclear weapons and troop movements.

Scientists will begin communication (similar to Morse code) with beings from other worlds, after receiving a signal from space.

Quantum physicists will find a way to connect with beings from other times as well.

By 2100, there will be regular trips to the moon, mainly to collect minerals. A mineral to be found there will prove invaluable. There are other, unexplained, activities happening on the moon and there will be rocket trips into space for fun.

The following future-life progression is from Dolores Cannon's subject, John. While featuring some similarities to others I mention regarding space travel, it includes significant differences. It post-dates a cataclysmic Earth Shift during which the Earth moved on its axis – with subsequent geological upheavals, flooding and depopulation – and includes friendly contact with extraterrestrials much earlier than mentioned elsewhere.

The environments recorded by Chet Snow and Helen Wambach in *Mass Dreams* and Dr. Wambach's conclusion that 95% of the population had been extinguished by 2100 also seem to post-date a cataclysm. It's possible that the 'mass dreams' reported by Snow and the future life reported by John, both in the 1980s, are on a different timeline from that foreseen in Weiss's and Jirsch's studies which were both undertaken in the new millennium, 20 years later.

John was progressed 100 years into the future, to 2087. He finds himself in the body of a woman, Zarea, on a spaceship manned by extraterrestrials, on a federation mission to their planet with several others from Earth, heading for Sirius, a star with 3 planets, taking crystals and the like to trade. Each member of the team has a different skill/ area to study. Zarea was born a natural healer and uses crystals, mental powers and visualization to heal. She is married to a man also on the mission who is going to study architecture and different methods of construction to get ideas for Earth.

The extraterrestrials are humanoid, pleasant looking, with golden brown skin and a bald cranium. They are friendly and caring and communicate telepathically. They have been interacting with humans for the last 80 years (since 2007). During the Earth Shift, contact was made with these ETs who have helped them form their new planetary centers (cities, but much smaller than the cities we now know). A new spaceport called 'Surveilas' east of Seattle is where UFOs land. Spaceships use electro-magnetic power collected in photovoltaic cells from the sun.

ETs also helped clear pollution of land and sea, healed people and showed them new technology. The polar icecaps are gone. A nuclear reactor on the Asian Islands (that used to be Asia) broke up in the Earth Shift and poisoned 300 square miles. None of this land can be used nor can it be flooded it as would pollute the ocean. ETs help Earth build its own power drives for vehicles and reinvent communications between islands.

There are approximately 120 million people left on Earth in 2087. Many died in the Earth Shift and resulting transition due to disease and deprivation. People regard attitudes before the shift as primitive as they are now more spiritually enlightened and know about their past lifetimes. Everyone unites in spiritual intercourse (prayer) to heal the planet.

Earth now has one World Government, formed in 2039, ten years after the shift, with its headquarters in Omaha. It is interested in the development of new colonies in space now there is no longer much land mass on Earth.

Earth has also been contacted by other extraterrestrials from Aldebaran, Betelgeuse and 2 other star systems. Earth is the newest member of the galactic federation, the requirement for membership of which is to understand the plan of the Creator and to be part of the galaxy-wide consciousness. The galactic federation has actually been influencing Earth since before the shift.

Cannon notes that John's vision of the future as Zarea may be only one possible future. Weiss's findings don't suggest a major event for 300-600 years, i.e. 2300 at the earliest. Contact with extraterrestrials is also foreseen much later, possibly 2250.

NDEr Mellen-Thomas Benedict believes that we will soon colonize other planets; and while he learned that we are not alone in the universe, the account of his NDE doesn't mention alien contact.

Space stations
Nostradamus foresaw a joint venture between the U.S., England and Russia to establish space stations on moon. This occurs between 2000 and 2100. There will be intelligent contact with extraterrestrials who will help with building space stations and colonization of space in the mid 22nd century. These will be established at the L5 points – this is the zone between the moon and Earth where the gravitational pull is equal from both directions, and thus less fuel needed to keep the station in position.

One of Dr. Weiss's clients, Patrick was progressed to a future time in the middle of the 23rd century, approximately 250 years from now. *A female in this future lifetime, who had to fight sexual discrimination to achieve her position, she works at an observatory, analyzing reports from space probes that relay messages from other planets in other galaxies. Earth also has a number of space stations orbiting throughout the solar system. From information collected so far, it seems there are dozens of other civilizations out there, but most are too far away for anything but an exchange of signals to let each other know of their existence. However, there are some closer contacts, with more advanced technology than that of Earth, who will be visiting soon.*

Much to Weiss's astonishment, a past-life regression of this same client revealed a past life from 60,000 years ago as a member of an alien civilization which travelled to Earth as its own world was dying. "When we arrive, others greet us, descendents of beings from earlier migrations from different star systems."

Similar in form to the inhabitants on Earth at that time, their intelligence is far superior, but they have chosen to aid the evolution of an evolving sub-species – human beings. While their souls could simply have chosen to be part of the reincarnation cycle, they wanted to preserve their knowledge and accomplishments. This client's task was to store that knowledge in secure hiding places that people will uncover at a time when they are able to understand it. (Dolores Cannon has also written about this.)

This client experienced a much later incarnation as an astronomer in Central or South America, so it is possible that this is where the aliens landed. His alien forbears were able to detach consciousness from the body at will and he reports that "Someday soon, your culture will learn how to do that, too."

(In order to please his parents and overcome what they considered an unhealthy obsession with science fiction, Patrick was an unhappy accountant. After his regression experiences, he decided to follow his passion and study astronomy. Weiss reports that on the astronomy course, he met his soulmate.)

Chet Snow, in a later commentary on his work with Wambach (see under Future Lifestyles) states that in 300 years some of the participants of their study saw themselves "in other places in space, other galaxies even. There is a legend in the Hopi Indians of Sedona that the last major project of the current civilisation is a 'platform in the sky.' This relates to the current establishment of a space docking station."

13. Technological advances

Like Weiss's comment of no major changes in the next 100 years, it very much appears that Jirsch's subjects, too, do not foresee any Earth Shift in the next 100 years – as their common vision is of a more developed society – although global warming and its resulting flooding is mentioned.

Due to pollution in the cities, governments will offer incentives for people to leave their cars at home. Many cities will adopt free or subsidized travel on high speed electric trains. Car companies develop small electric or hybrid cars. A super car will be developed which runs on very little fuel. These changes will be impelled as the quality of petrol and oil declines. Japan and some Middle Eastern countries will favor a flying car.

By 2055, fewer people own cars as high-speed electric trains provide clean, efficient transport. International travel is quicker and cleaner as planes now fly just outside the Earth's atmosphere. U.K. to Australia can be done in just over 2 hours.

By 2100, many will work from home or near their homes, using walkways and shuttle buses to get to work. Rather than travelling to conferences, advanced skyping technology is used.

Some study participants describe vast cities with walkways between buildings and small shuttles travelling at great speeds through tubes. These are fuel efficient and non-polluting. Some report a small pod-like vehicle (an advance on the electric car) that can take off vertically. It is non-polluting and sits outside the home on its own platform.

Other participants describe small towns, usually built along ley lines, like communal villages. Few people travel to other places as they are all much the same. Bicycles become more popular as people are more health and pollution conscious. Homes will be self-cleaning. Furnishings will be made of natural materials.

By 2100, Government buildings, e.g. the Pentagon and Houses of Parliament, military bases and sensitive locations, will be protected by some sort of energy wave – possibly already being developed today, but causing problems with whales, dolphins and migrating birds. Weapons will use lasers rather than artillery shells. 'Super' soldiers will be especially screened and trained from childhood.

Jirsch saw people carrying a stick-like object that with a flick of the wrist opens into a scroll. Operating with the insertion of a microchip, people are using these to read books, watch TV, email, text and look at and speak to others. They are used by students to access information, much like smartphone use today. (Children of the future laugh at the way people used pen and paper a century ago!) The sticks are activated by the owner's DNA to prevent theft and cut out as soon as someone else operates them.

Classroom teaching is a multi-sensory experience with advanced virtual reality programs (like the holodeck on the starship *Enterprise*). Teaching is geared to a student's personal strengths and vocational, creative, or sporting aptitudes. There is also greater emphasis on values: compassion, caring for others, and self-awareness and consequences. Children of the future are much less self-centered than today.

NDEr Dannion Brinkley saw the invention and implementation of a nanochip with the potential to be used for good or evil. (This has already been developed.) He was shown its implication in the finding of lost children or the tracking of missing military personnel in war. However, it could be used to monitor the activities of civilians, or to deliver a deadly virus into the body of an unsuspecting victim that a government wanted eliminated, or implanted in the elderly as a traceless form of euthanasia.

Astral traveler Bruce Moen was shown the development of a radio-like tuning device through which people could contact loved ones who have passed over. He was told that information from the other side would help prepare people for the changes to come. (Some years prior to this, in the early nineties, well-known NDE researcher Raymond Moody developed a 'psychomanteum' or scrying chamber which enabled contact with people in the afterlife.)

Computer technology

Nostradamus foresaw computers: "man giving up too much of his power to machines." He saw voice-activated and then thought-activated computers (which according to Cannon, the Japanese have now developed). These computers would be universal as it wouldn't matter which language you speak as the machine operates on messages from the mind. The final computer would be an organic computer, which would replicate and take care of itself, using protein and bacteria that can hold information.

Interestingly, in 1975 during his NDE, Dannion Brinkley was told that a biological engineer from the Middle East will find a way to alter DNA and create a biological virus that will be used in the manufacture of computer chips. In 1998, two Israeli researchers at the Israel Institute of Technology discovered a process in which strands of DNA are incorporated into a working electronic component.

Nostradamus also foresaw the World Wide Web – the world with strings or cords wrapped around it, all going into a central computer. According to Dolores Cannon, somewhere in Europe is a central computer called 'the Beast.' Coincidentally, or perhaps not, in the kabala (system of ancient Jewish numerology) of Nostradamus's time, 'world wide web' reduces to 666 (world=6, wide=6 web=6. Thus www = 666). In the future time that Nostradamus foresaw, everyone would be given a number in this machine (Rev. 13.16-18). These numbers would be inscribed on people's bodies and would provide access to information and resources. The elite would have numbers that gave them access to everywhere; lesser people would have controlled or limited access.

14. Cure for cancer/ Medical advances

According to Jirsch's study, by 2025 pollution will result in an increase in skin and breathing problems, including a new type of asthma that is resistant to drugs. Homeopathy proves to be the answer. By 2027, drug companies and governments will embrace natural remedies after evidence appears that some of today's drugs are in our water and causing health problems. Companies will be held accountable for additives in their products which have an adverse affect on health. Cures for cerebral palsy and multiple sclerosis will be found, as well as an expensive cure for some types of cancer, creating debate over healthcare, class and money.

One of the prophetic visions that NDEr Dannion Brinkley was shown during his first NDE was a battle for spiritual recognition that would take place within the healthcare system. The fight would be with technocrats over the control of our own healthcare and the right to chose alternative therapies. Brinkley was shown a new wave of medical equipment that boosts the healing powers of the body. He was told: "The body has a mind of its own and can heal itself. People must come to realize that." Mellen-Thomas Benedict has already developed 'phototherapy' devices using light to promote healing, and which also, he claims, promote anti-aging.

By 2055, Jirsch reports that people are generally healthier. Many illnesses have been cured or contained. There are fewer genetic and birth defects as babies can be treated in the womb. Spinal injuries will be reparable with a specially developed strong nylon-like surgical thread.

By 2100, there have been great advances in medicine. Most cancers have been eradicated and Aids is under control. From birth, people are health-profiled so that many illnesses are nipped in the bud. There are some new illnesses, however; mainly skin and lung diseases caused by irritants in the environment and pollution.

Future hospitals are now using colors, sounds and scents to create a comforting atmosphere. Surgery is simple, fast and non-invasive with even serious issues treated on an outpatient basis. Lasers have revolutionized medicine. With the beam often refined by passing through a crystal or diamond, lasers are used to repair wounds and bones and remove tumors and fat. Many of today's healers see themselves working with lasers and crystals in their future lives.

Brinkley was shown an operating room of the distant future. There were no scalpels; instead, patients were exposed to special lights that changed the vibration of cells within the body. According to the being accompanying Brinkley, every part of the body has its own vibratory rate and when the lights return the diseased organ to its proper vibration, healing takes place. Brinkley was shown cancer and other life-threatening diseases eradicated with healing wands made of light. Finally politicians and medical professionals are recognizing "that you cannot drug people to health." As one of the Spirit Beings Brinkley encountered during his NDE said, "If you don't use your spirit to heal, then you are not truly healed."

Jirsch foresees natural remedies in greater use. An antibiotic homeopathic remedy will be far more efficient than today's antibiotics, with no side effects. The sap of a new hybrid plant, something like a cross between a cactus and an orchid, provides a vitamin shot and immunity boost in one go. Subliminal recording will also be used to aid recovery.

Music will become very important – to enhance productivity, relaxation and feelings of love and sexuality; to lessen pain; to aid concentration and learning, intuition and creativity; and even to heighten strength. Music will be used to balance people with emotional problems and to stir the emotions of criminals – to promote awareness of the reason for their act and empathy for its effect on others.

There is much more emphasis on healthy living. People of today (present time) are regarded as weak and polluted due to all the toxins we ingest in our food! The people of the future are much more discerning when it comes to food, with great chefs being seen as artists.

15. Downfall of America/ Rise of other superpowers

The majority of NDE studies seem to come out of America, so this country features prominently. A number saw the destruction of New York or a possible terrorist attack. (This could possibly have been 9/11 in 2001). One noted that the views and lives of Americans would change as a result.

Howard Storm was shown a future where a massive worldwide depression would occur unless the U.S. changed its current manner of behavior. According to his 'friends' on the other side, the privilege of leading the world to a better age had been given to the U.S. – a country famously founded on spiritual principles. Two centuries later, in 1985, when Storm had his NDE, the example the Americans were setting in terms of overconsumption and production of weapons was not encouraging. Their message was uncompromisingly grim.

He reports "The U.S. has been given the opportunity to be the teacher for the world, but much is expected of those to whom much has been given. The U.S. has been given more of everything than any country in the history of the world and it has failed to be generous with those gifts. If the U.S. continues to exploit the rest of the world by greedily consuming the world's resources, the U.S. will have God's blessing withdrawn. [It] will collapse economically, which will result in civil chaos... You will have people killing people for a cup of gasoline. The world will watch in horror as your country is obliterated by strife. The rest of the world will not intervene because they have been victims of your exploitation... Today the U.S. is the primary merchant of war and the culture of violence that you export to the world. You have sown the seeds of your own destruction.

Either you will destroy yourselves or God will bring it to an end if there is no change... The U.S. must change immediately and become teachers of goodness and generosity to the rest of the world."

Ned Dougherty was shown the collapse of the U.S. economy and subsequent collapse of the government. During his second NDE several months after the first, Dougherty was given a similar message to Storm from a spiritual being he took to be the Archangel Michael. The message finishes with a dire vision for America in the new millennium: "to be reduced to piles of dust, to be covered over by the waters."

According to FLP therapist Anne Jirsch, there will be a stock market crash before 2025 which will badly affect America and Japan, with mass unemployment and economic migration.

By 2100 America is no longer a superpower. In fact it is described as "poor and no longer powerful." It had been involved in a big war about 50 years previously and is just coming out of a lengthy depression. Parts of the country are heavily polluted and unlivable. Cities are squalid. Many people are poor or have gone back to a happier, more rural way of life. The rich are even richer. With a new president, the U.S.A. is about to invest in new technology and pioneering science.

China

Jirsch reports that by 2100, China has become much more powerful than now, but the country is divided. People in western areas live in cramped conditions and water is short. The eastern side of the country is very high-tech with a high standard of living. A super-city has been constructed, with shuttle buses that run through tubes.

Cayce prophesized that in the distant future (date unspecified), China will become 'the cradle of Christianity' in its application of spiritual values, as that is its destiny. NDEr Ned Dougherty was told by the Lady of Light to pray for the conversion of China as a requirement for global peace.

Middle East
During his NDE in 1984, Dougherty was shown flashpoints throughout the Middle East and Europe representing areas where major acts of terrorism, aggression and war would be initiated by fanatical religious groups supposedly acting in the name of God. He was told that none of this was God's plan. After that, a series of earth-shattering geophysical changes occurred but he was told that they didn't need to happen if man got back on track and followed God's plan. (See Creating a Better Future for Dougherty's description of God's plan.)

Jirsch does not report geophysical changes. By 2055, oil has run out in the Middle East, conflict fades and peace returns. About a third of Africa will become uninhabitable due to searing heat. There will also be 'no go' zones where there is no governmental control.

Russia
Brinkley was shown the collapse of communism and told to: "Watch the Soviet Union. How the Russian people go, so goes the world. What happens to Russia is the basis for everything that will happen to the economy of the free world."

He was also shown a vision of himself and another man in the streets of Moscow watching long lines of hungry Russians lining up outside stores in the hope of buying whatever food was available. (This happened when he visited Moscow with Raymond Moody in 1992 just after the fall of communism.) He was shown that a leader from Russia would become a U.N. leader and also the rise of an environmental religion beginning in Russia.

Similarly, Cayce predicted: "On Russia's religious development will come the greater hope of the world." He suggested that this will happen when Russia and America unite harmoniously to combine Russia's abundant raw resources with America's technology.

Japan

A century hence, according to Jirsch's study, Japan has become the most technologically developed country of all. There is a high standard of living and it is clean and peaceful despite the large population. A huge earthquake has devastated many of its cities, but the Japanese have rebuilt beautiful new cities using solar and wind power whenever possible, incorporating trees and nature with moving pavements and underground trains.

U.K.

A century hence, the U.K. is smaller and rounder, with much land being lost to rising sea levels. The climate is now tropical with lush countryside and strange new animals and plants. Some cities have become no-go areas due to tribal wars between groups of different backgrounds. Village life has become preferable to city life. While the country isn't poor, internal trade in fish and commodities is the norm.

A young girl is queen, but the monarchy has little influence. Football is still popular. Huge crowds watch hi-tech sports games that combine physical ability with electronic equipment. Winning carries great status. Television now has thousands of channels and is more interactive. There is greater emphasis on children learning social skills as there had been a worrying time when home entertainment and insularity had led to people becoming isolated, socially inept and depressed.

16. Global unification

According to Nostradamus, countries will unite after the Earth Changes in order to survive. All present governments will fall. There will be vigilantism and military law as people recover. Present-day countries will no longer exist, replaced instead by small duchies and kingdoms (groups of people banding together for mutual cooperation). The U.S. will be governed by a small council of people of high integrity and knowledge.

Sometime between 2000 and 2100 there will be the formation of a world government. Similarly, Dolores Cannon's subject, John, foresees one world government forming in the decade following the Earth Shift.

Other sources don't mention world government as such, but Jirsch's subjects report that by the middle of the 22nd century (around 2150) due to the evolved awareness of the unity of mankind, the concept of national identity and cultural differences is unimportant. Also due to travel and the increase of multiculturalism in preceding decades, national boundaries have become less important.

Jirsch gives the example of Jenny, who in 150 years' time is working in a remote scientific outstation. When asked about her co-workers and where they come from, she is uninterested in talking about their background and their past. Even in their downtime, they discuss the progress of their work. "This project is vitally important to plant life, and if we can achieve our aims, we will greatly enhance the quality of our plants and food sources. We will be making the world healthier, so why would we want to talk about things long since past?"

In this future, priorities are different. People are more interested and excited about the common good. There seems to be no desire for people to focus on their individual differences. Being part of the whole is more important.

17. Future lifestyles

In the 1980s, Drs. Helen Wambach, Leo Sprinkle and Chet Snow conducted dozens of group workshops across America and France, resulting in nearly four hundred future-life progressions. These were collated by Snow after Wambach's death and published in *Mass Dreams of the Future: Group*

Progressions to the Twenty-Second and Twenty-Fourth Centuries (1989).

Interestingly, about five per cent of subjects reported they were androgynous in 2100, with this figure rising to six per cent in 2300. (NDEr Mellen-Thomas Benedict, who foresaw the next 400 years, also reported that in the future the majority of people will be androgynous, neither male nor female, but having the characteristics of both. He also saw a lifespan of up to 150 years.) Snow established that average life spans in both periods seemed to be more or less the same as today.

But by far the most interesting aspect of Snow's analysis was the emergence of different types of life experience that were, broadly speaking, common to both future periods. He categorized these into:

Type I – living in a traveling spaceship, a space station or a protected colony on a nearby planet like Mars (later moving further afield into other galaxies)
Type II – living in spiritually evolved, new-age communities in predominantly mountain or coastal environments on Earth
Type III – living in usually enclosed (domed), high-technology, city environments on Earth
Type IV – living a relatively backward life usually in small rustic communities on Earth.

The **Type I (Space) and III (High Tech)** experiences were somewhat linked as high-technology cities on Earth acted as home base for many of the space travelers. Both types indicated that contact and cooperation with extraterrestrials was commonplace. A degree of continuation of a family-style life was reported by both. Type I (Space) respondents tended to be slightly more fulfilled by their scientific work, but many also reported boredom and isolation, brought on by the dominance of technology.

Type III (High Tech/ domed city) lifestyles predominantly focused on survival. Dissatisfaction and crime were rampant while art, literature and other humanistic aspects barely featured in their automated society. Most reported that there was no greenery or vegetation. If they left their enclosed cities they had to wear suits that protected them from the sun's radiation, as well as full breathing apparatus because the atmosphere was poisonous – and that if these failed they died. Their purely functional domed cities were often built partially underground or even under water.

This sounds very similar to the negative future that Weiss's client, John, foresaw: "*Technology accidents have made many areas uninhabitable. Farms and forests have disappeared and people live in huge city-states... Science and technology have advanced, as often for ill as for good, but human ambition and prejudices have not changed.*" In his positive future, he is in a very different environment, where they "*look for ways to create unity among people by encouraging an emphasis on similarities, not differences...*" – possibly Type II below.

For **Type II (New Age)**, part of their spiritual development was to coordinate their limited use of technology with their natural environment – there being a suggestion that they were able to maintain their pleasant habitats by their spiritual approach, while many other parts of the planet remained virtually uninhabitable. Their diet consisted of natural fruits and vegetables, and their average life spans had increased to over ninety years of age. A few reported that they used telepathy to communicate and that they could 'vacate' their bodies if they chose once their life tasks were completed.

According to NDEr Ned Dougherty, "There will be a great shift in the location of populated areas as a result of both the geophysical and geopolitical changes [to come]. Coastal and other low-lying and unstable areas will diminish in population, while mountainous and other stable areas become more desirable. Spiritually-minded people will be drawn together to create new self-supporting and self-sustaining communities. These pioneers of vision who are attuned to God's plan for mankind will be the architects for the brave new world that God has envisioned for our future."

Type IV (Rustic) reported a reversion to a relatively backward nineteenth-century existence in small communities – usually in a rural or small town environment, but occasionally in ruined cities. Meat-eaters, they led largely uncomplicated lives, with neither spiritual emphasis nor technology.

The progressions to 2300 and beyond were in many ways similar. By this time, there is an estimated population of around 2 billion. The proportion of Type I (Space) lifestyles had increased, largely due to colonization of planets outside our solar system. Domed structures were often mentioned, but in many cases these planets had an atmosphere and vegetation similar to Earth. Lives of those in spaceships, space stations and enclosed colonies on planets within our solar system continued to be somewhat lonely. However, those on planets in other parts of the galaxy were more family-oriented and fulfilling and in many cases spiritual.

The lives of the Type II (New Age) subjects continued much as before except in some cases the relatively small community settlements had expanded into major population centers with more modern technology but without losing their fundamental spirituality. There were hints from some that their higher vibrational state had made them less densely physical, and extraterrestrial contacts for these people often had a strong spiritual dimension. (This might explain the ambiguity in descriptions of 'Watchers' and 'spiritual guardians' described in the previous section on contact with aliens.)

Although more than half of the Type III (High Tech) subjects continued to live in enclosed cities because of the still-polluted atmosphere, by 2300 a significant minority reported that the atmosphere in their part of the globe was safe. These latter also reported that their lives were more fulfilling and even spiritual. A process of convergence between the Type II (New Age) and III (High Tech) lifestyles was at least partially underway by 2300. Meanwhile, apart from an apparent increase in the size of their communities, the Type IV (Rustic) lifestyle seemed pretty much unchanged.

Many of the Type II, III and IV respondents from both time periods reported living in various still-identifiable parts of the globe that overlap considerably. Ian Lawton and other commentators conclude that the two mutually exclusive atmospheric environments reported in the future (space and cities/ coast and rural) suggest the possibility of at least two alternative futures: one apocalyptic, the other spiritual.

18. Not the end of the world

There is no mention of the world ending in any of my sources. Nostradamus's prophecies end at 3797, but there is no suggestion that that is when the world will end.

We all know the world didn't end in 2012! According to the NASA website, the 'end of the world' notion was based on a huge misconception. The story started in 1995 with Nancy Leider, a woman claiming to have contact with ETs who warned her that a planetary object would sweep through the solar system causing a pole shift in the Earth that would destroy most of humanity. This catastrophe was initially predicted for May 2003, but when nothing happened, internet doomsday groups moved the date forward to December 2012 to link it with the end of one of the cycles in the ancient Mayan calendar – the winter solstice in 2012. Hence the predicted doomsday date of December 21, 2012.

Dolores Cannon in the *Three Waves of Volunteers and the New Earth* offers another explanation for the focus on 2012. According to the Mayan Calendar, the world has two trees (timelines?) and a new world tree is being created by those of us changing our consciousness. Dolores describes two Earths that will separate, (I'm guessing this means diverging timelines), and that 2012 will be the beginning of this separation.

Prepare yourselves for this next bit – it's pretty crazy! Clients under regression tell her that we've caused emotional (and consequently environmental) pollution on such a scale that it is affecting other universes and other dimensions (because we are all connected to everything through the Source). Beings close to the Source are stepping in. Because they can't do too much or it would interfere with the original 'free will directive,' they are trying to change things from within. The call went out for volunteers to incarnate and try to steer us back on track. Some volunteers are from other dimensions and alien races and have never incarnated on Earth before.

Thanks to the efforts of the volunteers and 'Watchers' from 'the other side', all of us living on Earth have already had our vibrations raised to a much greater extent than would have otherwise occurred. Things have improved to the extent that we will no longer destroy the Earth, but it needs to take a new path. There is going to be a dimensional shift, whereby one version of Earth will carry on much as is, with people of a lower vibration working out their karma the slow way, and the other will contain people of higher vibration, living more enlightened lives, ultimately evolving as light beings and having no karma. Bizarre as this sounds, it is similar to future visions reported by Jirsch further on (see 23. Evolution of humanity).

Ian Lawton also believes that 2012 signals a spiritual awakening. It's just possible that 2012 might be what Nostradamus refers to as a 'nexus point' – event of major impact – and that this nexus point might not be a physical event but the tipping point of a change in consciousness – 'the hundredth monkey phenomenon,' (Ken Keyes, *The Hundredth Monkey, 1982*).

This is the view of Mellen-Thomas Benedict who believes the pole shift is a shift in consciousness. He claims that while 2012 signals a paradigm shift to a 'higher energy,' the real pivotal moment comes around 2020 to 2040. We are entering into a greater awareness that we each create our own reality. Because of the nature of self-fulfilling prophecies, he cautions against buying into end-of-the-world thinking. As he discovered, your worldview creates your world.

19. Spiritual evolution/ Psychic powers

Many sources predict psychic or spiritual evolution with a corresponding development in mind powers – intuition (accessing information from the Source), healing (greater understanding of matter and energy), telepathy (including contact with people 'on the other side'), and even control over the weather. Ned Dougherty and Mellen-Thomas Benedict were both told that humankind would evolve into a new and more spiritually transformed race of beings.

The Cayce readings foretell that humanity's consciousness is evolving into a 'fifth root race' that would mark the golden age to come and a new understanding of humanity's relationship to God. (See 23. Evolution of humanity.)

Bruce Moen was similarly told that the change of consciousness mankind is undergoing is the opening up to the expression of pure unconditional love. This has been hastened/ facilitated by our Creator and will also open our minds to the multidimensional nature of our existence. Consequently, we will shed many beliefs about our supposed physical limitations.

According to Jirsch, by 2100, psychic skills have assumed more prominence in the mainstream of life. They will be used by police and governments, so a way to assess their abilities has been developed. *In Mass Dreams*, Chet Snow foresaw the emergence of clans or tribes of people born with enhanced telepathic and other psychic powers.

After the long years of devastation by natural and man-made earth changes as well as wars, Nostradamus saw a period of human renaissance unparalleled in our history. "People will be brought back to the Source. They will realize from whence they sprang and where they are going. This is when the time of healing will take place. People will become more mature spiritually and be able to heal themselves and heal the world, going much further in preparing to join the community of the 'Watchers' [extraterrestrials and spiritual beings who are keeping an eye on humanity's development]."

'The Great Genius'
In the mid-21st century, Nostradamus predicts the emergence of a great scientific genius who will help rebuild human society. (Quoting Dolores Cannon, from *Conversations*): "This man... will be one of the highest, most developed geniuses ever to appear in our present history of man. He... made the decision to use his genius to help rather than to hurt mankind... One of the things he envisions... is self-contained, self-supporting space stations... It was very easy for him [Nostradamus] to spot this man along the nexus of time paths because he creates such a large ultimate effect... This man is one of the major forces who will help the earth recover from the scars of war." (This is a war Nostradamus predicted would be started by 'the Antichrist,' a megalomaniac whose rise to power appears to have been averted on our present timeline. Hopefully, the Great Genius will still turn up!)

This great genius will be influential in pointing out the mistaken premises that today's science has built itself on. His ability to perceive scientific truths will cause major breakthroughs in our technological capabilities. "[He will] make clear the connections between the physical universe and the metaphysical universe as dealt with by religions." Because of these great advances, Nostradamus describes a time when a majority of people will be aware of higher powers and energies.

Weiss reports that by 3000, humans will have 'lighter,' less dense bodies and can communicate telepathically. Mind powers seem to be much more advanced. There is no evidence of anger, hatred or fear as people seem much more connected to their spiritual nature.

20. Changed attitude to death

Mellen-Thomas Benedict was told that population increase is getting very close to the optimal range of energy to cause a shift in consciousness. That shift in consciousness will change politics, money and energy. Our experiments with DNA will soon enable us to live as long as we want in our current bodies. However, after 150 years or so, (nowhere near as long as some of the ancients from Biblical days who were still begetting children at that age and not dying until they reached 800 plus), he reports that we will want to:

"...change channels. Living forever in one body is not as creative as reincarnation... We are actually going to see the wisdom of life and death, and enjoy it," knowing that we have already been alive forever. Our souls are eternal and the particles that make up the body have also been alive forever. They come from the unending Stream of Life that recycles itself eternally.

Ned Dougherty was shown a scene of the future, "several decades after the year 2000," in which tropical and non-tropical plants and trees grew side by side due to the geophysical changes on Earth in the intervening years. The climate was warm and nature pulsated with a healing universal energy. In a dwelling were a dying man and his son, who were communicating that they had had a wonderful life together even though they had had many hardships. There was no sadness between them as, in this new era of mankind, death was recognized as the transition between the soul's journey on Earth and the spiritual afterlife. "It was one of many changes that separated the new world from the old." This final vision assured Dougherty that this world has a wonderful future.

Another NDEr, Howard Storm, was shown a similar vision of people, 200 years from now, accepting death as a natural release of the spirit to heaven when they felt their life experience had been completed. He saw the community celebrating – much as at a graduation ceremony.

In the Wambach-Snow study of future lifestyles, Snow reports that, in general, by 2300, attitudes to death have changed completely, with most people fully realizing it is just a transition to another state. As a result, reports of choosing to leave a body that was worn out, or because all tasks for that life had been accomplished, were commonplace among all types (Space, New Age, Hi-tech and Rustic).

21. Religious reformation

During Nostradamus's time, the Catholic Church wielded considerable power in France through the Inquisition. His family was originally Jewish, but forced to be baptized and become Catholic or be killed. They had to choose a new name, hence Nostradamus. Naturally Nostradamus was deeply unhappy about this. He prophesized that the Catholic Church would collapse from within – it was "built on sand." The last pope, in our time, would be assassinated which would herald the downfall of the church. In time, he foresaw that religion would return to what it was supposed to do – no dogma, rules about sin, etc., but the way of Jesus – meetings in people's homes, sharing insights and healings. The image of Jesus on the cross would no longer be worshipped, as in this future time it is seen as a symbol of barbarism and death.

Jirsch foresees a future Catholic resurgence and adds that by 2100, there will be many more religious movements. Mainstream Islam has turned against fanatics, with its followers promoting world peace. Religious aggression was also prophesied by one NDEr, one religion against another, but eventually a reformation in spirituality as religions become 'enlightened.'

22. Hidden knowledge revealed

Both Cayce and Nostradamus report that archaeologists will discover secrets hidden in the pyramids. Cayce describes a Hall of Records that will be discovered in Egypt between the sphinx and the great pyramid just before the Earth Changes, but after humanity has attained a higher level of spirituality.

Atlanteans hid the records of man's origins – when Spirit first took form 4.5 billion years ago – and his advances. Sometime in the far distant past, aware that their civilization was about to be destroyed, the Atlanteans made 3 copies of their records and hid them in Bimini, Egypt and the Yucatan peninsula in Mexico (an important area for the Mayan civilization before the Spanish conquest). Eventually all of these hiding places will be uncovered (quite possibly by reincarnations of the old Atlanteans who have achieved a level of spiritual growth that would enable them to understand the information they find).

23. Evolution of humanity

FLP therapist Anne Jirsch reports that in the future. there will be two types of humans – those who have evolved spiritually, who she refers to as 'Trans People' – people who have evolved far beyond what they are now; and those she calls 'Grunters,' who live for the moment and have no spiritual awareness. Some souls even evolve to the extent that they lose their human form and become 'Light Beings.'

For some time she was unaware of the Grunters and came to realize this was because the people who came to her workshops or sessions were on a spiritual path, and once on it made great strides, their future lifetimes often far in excess, spiritually, of this one. By the next century, the world is a very different place technologically; and attitudes, views and morals have advanced considerably.

Trans People – those who connect and contribute
Trans People are less concerned with self than the majority of people today and have learned to connect more to others. They have realized that they are part of a 'collective consciousness' – that by hurting or helping another, you hurt or help yourself. As part of a wider unity, these people are emotionally stronger and more stable. They are more sensitive to energy and can feel another's energy from a long distance. Our future selves also tend to be lighter in weight, taller, stronger, leaner and more similar to each other. (This description possibly reflects the androgyny of our future selves reported by both Wambach and Benedict.)

For Trans People, their emotional investment is not in their immediate relationship with another or the state of their finances, but in their work and their contribution to the human race as a whole. (NDEr Benedict says that one of the signs of spiritual advancement on Earth is when you see truly enlightened beings entering into the Fortune 500 List. This has already begun with the example set by billionaires Bill and Melinda Gates, Mark Zuckerberg, Warren Buffet and Michael Bloomberg who founded the Giving Pledge in 2010 and have been joined by nearly 200 others committed to giving most of their wealth to philanthropic causes.)

Grunters – those who live for themselves
This subspecies, as Jirsch refers to them, are people who live for the moment and are not spiritually aware. She cites evidence of this division already in the work of evolutionary theorist Dr. Oliver Curry, who believes that as a result of people being choosier about their sexual partners humanity will, over the next 1000 years, divide into two species he labels as 'gracile' and 'robust.'

Shirley MacLaine, well known for her books documenting her spiritual search, mentions in *I'm Over All That (2011),* that while she was in Peru in 1987 shooting *Out on a Limb,* the Peruvian shamans told her that a new species of Homo sapiens was about to appear. They called the new humans 'Homo luminous.' "They told me that the forerunners of Homo luminous were already among us. They would possess qualities that we do not now have."

Dolores Cannon, in her penultimate book, (*The Three Waves of Volunteers and the New Earth*), describes two separate paths for the Earth, reporting a shifting of vibration that is currently taking place in which people with humanitarian values will experience a different Earth (or reality) from people who pursue only materialistic and selfish goals.

Earth is referred to as a great experiment, in that humans have been allowed to evolve with no direct knowledge of their Source (or that they are part of a universal consciousness). So far mankind as a whole doesn't seem to have done a great job of evolving his/her spiritual nature in order to reconnect with that Source, so, according to Cannon, more spiritually advanced beings are reincarnating to bring us to greater awareness of the values that create unity and connection.

Light beings/ Spiritual guides

As well as the 'trans people' and the 'grunters,' a third type of being comes into greater prominence further into the future (24th century). Spiritual helpers, angels, have been mentioned since biblical times; and as Jirsch reminds us, there is a wealth of stories in the public arena from people who have had contact with angelic beings. ('Angel' in Hebrew and Greek means 'messenger.')

Jirsch reports that some of her clients describe themselves in future lives as translucent or shimmering or not in human form. Puzzled clients would report that they weren't sure if they were male or female. *"I just seem to be a ball of light."* Or *"I am really light and floaty, almost like a fairy."*

Jirsch herself experienced something similar during one of her own FLPs. *In this future time, she was in a spacecraft that was about to land at a base on a planet that wasn't Earth. It was all very routine, so obviously the planet had been colonized for some time. She felt lighter, almost floating, and connected to everybody and the environment, which made her feel strong and secure.* Her current self seemed heavy and primitive in comparison, and this is what inspired her to develop the techniques to bring back from the future some of the awareness of our more evolved selves.

One of her clients, Ed, had a similar experience. In his current life, he is a leading self-development trainer and wanted to know where he was heading. Under FLP he reports: "I am in some sort of a temple, but there is no floor. It seems to be floating through space." Answering questions from Jirsch, he says that he is neither male nor female, but formless, made of energy. There are others there like him. They communicate telepathically, not through talking. His role is teaching and guiding. "From here, I can reach many people but I also travel. Wow, I can change form. I can become more solid when I need to. It depends on who I am teaching."

Another client, aware she is female, reports that her role is also to guide people. She lives in a cold climate and wears a tunic made of synthetic fibers that have a natural thermostat to keep the wearer cool in the warm and warm in the cold. She doesn't eat food. Instead she says she feeds off the light. "It gives us peace and growth and energy."

Jirsch reports that the light beings of the future tend to assist not just our species, but others on other planets as well. In this lifetime, they are usually already working in a spiritual field as healers, psychics or advanced practitioners of meditation.

In a final case study, Jirsch describes the FLP of a female scientist, Rohini, who currently works conducting drug trials, but whose goal is to work with natural, holistic remedies. Interestingly, in her life just past she had been a drug trafficker, but in this life she was putting drugs to good use.

In her next life, she has evolved even further. She travels 300 years into the future. A young woman with a human form that appears to be floating "like an angel," she is a hostess for people who have come to her planet on a pilgrimage of self-development, having completed their life's work. The planet is similar to Earth but has a higher vibration. Everyone communicates telepathically.

Rohini says that she needs to be close to the sun as it is her energy source. She visits other planets, including Earth. It seems that she also has the ability to go back in time to help people there as her work is to "prevent car accidents in the dimension and time you exist in now. I touch people on the shoulder when they fall asleep at the wheel. I know when something is going to happen. I like doing this, but I do not like the Earth connection... There is too much pain."

24. Time travel

As Jirsch's client Rohini reports above, time travel is on the cards in 300 years time – but for altruistic purposes, not (as one might suppose) to find hidden treasure or to change the past!

Hypnotherapist, Dr. Bruce Goldberg, has been investigating future-life progression since the 1980s. Much of the focus of his work seems to be directed to visitations by time travelers from the future (his explanation for UFOs and alien abductions). He claims these 'chrononauts' – not aliens – come from between 1000 and 3000 years in the future and have mastered teleportation. In his book *Past Lives, Future Lives Revealed,* Goldberg says these time travelers are with us now and that their main purpose is not to abduct us for genetic study, but to accelerate our spiritual development so that we (humans in the future) can ascend to God. He also mentions visitations by various sorts of aliens, some less friendly than others. (I have not encountered mention of chrononauts or unfriendly aliens in other material I have read.)

25. The far future

The following comment is representative of that made by many NDErs who were shown the future: "After the darkest hour had passed away, during which time all the former things of this world had disintegrated and decayed, I saw a new consciousness emerging and humanity evolving in a new form. Thereafter, I beheld a Golden Age in which people would live in love and harmony with each other and all of nature."

(www.near-death.com/science/research/future.html)

After a time of turmoil, Cayce, Nostradamus and Dr. George Ritchie, (*Return from Tomorrow, 1978*), prophesy 1000 years of peace.

Chet Snow in *Mass Dreams of the Future* refers to a period after 2300 AD, described as 'the Outward Wave,' when humanity will no longer be bound either by this solar system or by present-day concepts of 3D reality.

Even further into the future, 1000 years from now, according to Jirsch, we will be multidimensional, using and understanding energy in ways that are beyond us now.

One of Brian Weiss's clients, progressed to the distant future, at least 1000 years from now, reports: "People don't need bodies any more, though they can have them if they wish. We can go anywhere and be anyone by using visualization and thought. We communicate through consciousness and also through auras. The earth is very lush and green. I can't see many people, but this may be because most don't wish to have bodies; they are happy being consciousness and light.

"The world is a transcendentally peaceful place, with no hint of war, violence, misery or grief. I've been able to scan the planet for negative emotions; none exist." He concludes by saying that his choices alone won't produce that future. It is the collective decisions of all humans that will get us there.

CREATING A BETTER FUTURE

"The mind is the builder. I encourage my clients to work now, in the present, on the pathways they are forming which will build their future." – Dr. Chet Snow

What can one person do?

Some NDErs were given explicit instructions about what they needed to do to improve the state of things and some were given more general messages that would apply to all of us.

Howard Storm asked the light beings how to change things on Earth when it meant changing the behavior of so many people. The beings replied that "all it takes to make a change was one person. One person trying, and then, because of that, another person changing for the better. They said that the only way to change the world was to begin with one person. One will become two, which will become three, and so on. That's the only way to effect a major change."

It seems that every good cause has started with the actions of just one person. In a moment of inspiration back in 1982, Ann Herbert wrote "Practice random kindness and senseless acts of beauty" on a restaurant table mat. The man next to her wrote it down. It became a worldwide phenomenon as people were attracted to the idea.

On television recently was a story about a reformed gang member learning to knit in prison and teaching other prisoners how to make sleeping mats for the homeless out of recycled plastic shopping bags. "You can't help everyone, but everyone can help someone – and the streets in winter are cold and hard."

Work at what you love

Dannion Brinkley was told to present 'spiritualistic capitalism 'to the world. Rather than having 'getting an income' as a goal, each one of us needs to find something we love to do and then using that talent or gift to serve the world while also making an income. Similarly, Mellen-Thomas Benedict says, "the future is not just about having a job but about expressing who you truly are."

Prayer – a mighty arsenal

Ned Dougherty, after being shown catastrophic visions of the future, was told that "the world could be saved, not by its leaders, but by prayer groups throughout the world. I was told that the prayers of a group of twenty could save a nation from war." He says, "Prayer is the most powerful weapon in the arsenal of humanity... **Prayer will arm us with the power to suspend the natural laws to avoid geophysically cataclysmic events."**

According to John van Auken of A.R.E., the Edgar Cayce official website, Cayce stated that none of the physical devastation he predicted *has* to happen. The stability of the planet lies in humanity's collective hands. Cayce also confirmed the biblical axiom that 10 good people can save an entire city (Gen. 18.32). He quotes an old story told by the editor of *Guideposts* (an inspirational magazine still available today) who received letters from two women in a small town in California. Each told him how they were awakened in the night and were powerfully guided by Spirit to go out into the street of their little town and pray, which they did. Around 5 a.m., a terrifying earthquake hit their town, destroying the entire downtown area, but not one person was killed or injured. These two ladies didn't know each other, living on opposite sides of the town. However, the prayers of two saved a town.

Van Auken advises, "Rather than get anxious over the world situation and [blame or lobby] political leaders, prayer is a powerful service we can perform for our fellow planet dwellers. Our prayers ascend into the Collective Consciousness and subliminally affect the whole of human consciousness and nature's sensitive vibrations. As Cayce advised, 'Why worry when you can pray? He [God] is the Whole, you are a part. Coordinate your abilities with the Whole.'"

In 1970, the whole world united in prayer when Houston had a problem. Both the Senate and House passed resolutions asking all Americans to pray at 9 o'clock Eastern standard time for the safe return of their countrymen. They also urged businesses and communications media to pause for prayers at that hour if they could. The prayer went around the world and the movie *Apollo 13* depicted its extraordinary results. In August 2017, this happened again, with prayers for Houston from around the world, after news of the devastating floods caused by Hurricane Harvey.

Water researcher, Dr. Masaru Emoto called for worldwide prayer after the Fukushima nuclear disaster in the wake of the magnitude 9 earthquake in 2011 and has also initiated other projects for prayer and peace. Both the Unity movement and Self Realization Fellowship have a worldwide prayer circle dedicated to worldwide harmony and individuals renewing their connection with the divine Source.

In *Embraced by the Light,* Betty Eadie describes how she saw angels rushing to answer prayers and explains that prayers must be a demonstration of faith and gratitude. Doubt creates a barrier to their fulfillment. (For advice on constructive prayer, see metaphysician Florence Shovel Shinn's *The Game of Life,* available free on the internet.)

God's plan

During his NDE, Ned Dougherty was told by a 'Lady of Light' that none of the dreadful visions of war and devastation he was shown would occur if mankind began to recognize and work with God's plan. "The fate of mankind rest[s] on our ability, individually and collectively, to change the direction of mankind in accordance with God's plan."

Dougherty was shown a movie of scenes of his future – the plan that God had intended for him; scenes totally incongruent with the life he had been leading before his NDE: writing a book that would be a source of inspiration for many; speaking in a university auditorium to doctors, medical researchers and students; visiting Egypt, meeting with political leaders (all of which he did many years after his NDE). He was warned that the messages he was communicating would be the subject of much criticism by organizations who were more motivated by fear and control than by open-mindedness.

Dougherty also watched scenes where he visited the bedsides of the sick and dying to comfort them with his messages, rewarding for both them and himself as he developed new insights. "I recognized that the greatest rewards in life do not come from seeking material riches and physical comfort, but from performing acts of caring and kindness for others."

Bruce Moen was told by the alien beings he encountered that the sign he was given of God's plan underway (a comet in the sky) was given not to him as an individual human, but as a representative of all humans. "Human consciousness has a widespread intention to move past its limiting, physical existence to expand into a new home you would call nonphysical... The Earth Changes alignment [with the Source of Pure Unconditional Love] is increasing the capacity in humans to experience and express Love."

Service

This is God's plan in a nutshell. Brinkley says, "The quickest way to change to world is to be of service to others. Show that your love can make a difference in the lives of people and thereby someone else's love can make a difference in your life. By each of us doing that and working together we change the world one inner person at a time."

FLP and past-life regression therapist, Chet Snow agrees: "The new energy on the planet is about service, but not in a servile way. Be each other's servant, each giving your best and receiving the best from others."

Asking for spiritual help

Dougherty was given a message by the spiritual beings he encountered in the afterlife. At one stage he encountered what can only be described as 'a heavenly host,' thousands of spiritual beings who viewed his life review and future scenes with him. While Dougherty states, "There are no secrets in the spiritual realms," there is no judgment either. The beings told him: "We stand ready to come to your aid when you need us, and you will. Call us. We will flock to you when the time comes."

When Dougherty helped organize an anti-drug event in his hometown after his recovery, he saw these beings in the sky above the event. He "realized that we embodied humans are never alone." These spiritual beings are always around us, working to inspire, protect and guide us to recognize and perform our mission in life.

Betty Eadie, *Embraced by the Light,* saw the same thing: "I saw the earth with its billions of people on it. I saw them scrambling for existence... I saw the angels hovering above them... to help and give direction and protection. I saw that we could literally call down thousands of angels in our aid if we ask in faith. We are all precious and carefully watched over."

Unity

Howard Storm was told, "They [spiritual beings/ messengers] want every person to consider every other person greater than their own flesh. They want everyone to love everyone else, completely; more, even, than they love themselves. If someone, someplace in the world hurts, then we should hurt; we should feel their pain. And we should help them. Our planet has evolved to the point, for the first time in our history, that we have the power to do that. We are globally linked. And we could become one people."

It was interesting to note that none of the messages that NDErs brought back was about worshipping God or building churches; rather it was about honoring ourselves, others and our shared home, Earth. Many spoke of the Light – life, energy, love – that flows through all of creation and the 'enlightenment' that needs to occur, in fact will occur, one way or another. They shared a concept of a universal God, not as separate and above but within and throughout.

HOW TO CHOOSE YOUR BEST FUTURE

"Most people don't really need help, from a psychic or a psychologist, in solving their problems. I remind them of what the Beings of Light told me about humans, that we are all great and powerful spiritual beings who sometimes forget our own spiritual strengths. "Just for a few minutes put aside all of the petty things that go on in your job, ignore the way your kids are acting, put all of your baggage with your spouse on hold, and try to look at your spirit, or think of something you love. If you try to please your spirit, which is your real self, then most decisions are not that tough to make. You can sometimes see the possible future when you do that. It is when you try to please everyone in your life instead of your spiritual self that you end up in spiritual crisis."

Dannion Brinkley (*At Peace in the Light*)

EFFECT OF KNOWING THE FUTURE

The effect of future visions for both NDErs and progression subjects was that most of them changed their lives. FLP therapists Brian Weiss and Anne Jirsch both report that participants felt a new sense of peace after viewing the future and learning that it wasn't such a bad place. Everyday worries about climate change, wars and the environment faded as participants were spurred to do what they could to bring the good changes forward in time. They joined environmental groups, recycled or made more use of public transport.

One of Jirsch's clients, Jude, saw herself in a future life sending vast and brilliant energy to trouble-spots on Earth. In one scene, a group of villagers had fled their homes to a cave in the mountains to escape war. Jude could see herself sending energy to light up the cave. Several weeks later, when Jude's daughter was having problems with aggression from a wayward stepchild, Jude, powerless to help in any substantial way, decided to fill their home with the same energy she had witnessed herself sending in a future life. She imagined light around herself and then expanding to fill the room, her house, and outward until it travelled to the stepchild's sleepout.

As the light reached the sleepout, Jude had a vision of the step-child reacting with violence, throwing things about as if trying to resist the light. So she sent even more brilliant waves of light into the room. She didn't expect much from her visualization so was astonished when she visited the next day and saw her daughter and stepchild interacting harmoniously as if nothing had ever happened.

SUMMARY: WHAT HAVE WE LEARNED?

There is more than one possible future

All sources agree that the future is not fixed. Rather, common visions of the future indicate that certain events, e.g. disasters, colonization of space, are *likely*. In addition, different visions of the future in the same timeframe indicate that there is a range of possible future paths, or timelines (from optimal to catastrophic), in which disasters are experienced to a greater or lesser degree, and the timing of events may differ – or perhaps not even happen – depending on mankind's actions now.

There are also critical times – nexus points – when a major event in the evolution of human consciousness causes the timeline, or future path, to diverge significantly, shifting from one timeline to another. Several sources agree a shift occurred most recently in 2012.

Natural disasters can be ameliorated

Almost all sources see a greatly reduced world population (from billions to millions) at some time in the near future. The cause is unclear – the issues of pollution and fertility are mentioned by some. A more likely cause of the population plummet is the frequently mentioned global catastrophe: a pole shift or significant climate change causing melting of the icecaps and worldwide flooding – with perhaps only 10% of land remaining. The climatic events that are said to herald these earth changes are becoming more obvious.

A surprising common report is that the many natural disasters we are now experiencing are not 'Acts of God' but the consequence of the cumulative effect on nature of man's negative emotions. In fact, a number of sources warn of a catastrophic global disaster (Nostradamus, Cayce, Wambach and Snow, and many NDErs), which it seems that humanity has brought upon itself through lack of brotherhood, aggression, and the selfish consumerism of modern civilization. However, this has not occurred within the predicted timeframe of most sources.

It is even possible that the shift in the Earth's axis predicted by both Nostradamus and Cayce has already occurred – in the 2011 quake that hit Japan; its effects ameliorated due to the various altruistic movements (human rights, peace, civil rights, New Age, environmental, social and animal welfare, etc) that have taken place since WW2. While the 20,000 deaths in the subsequent tsunami and the massive fatalities that continue with quakes and volcanic eruptions around the world are not to be taken lightly, *global* population devastation from this cause at least appears to have been averted.

Technology gives way to nature

At least two sources foresee a brighter immediate future (Jirsch and Weiss). However, Weiss reports "dark times" further down the track – in about 300 years (outside the scope of Jirsch's study) – but this time may be approaching more rapidly.

On this non-catastrophic timeline, the near future promises technological and medical advances pretty much as expected: petrol-free cars, space travel, cures for cancer and MS, along with a move away from drugs to natural remedies, light- and music-based therapies, and a greater recognition that physical ailments are the product of neglecting the spirit.

The emergence of a strong environmental movement to deal with pollution is almost universally predicted. If this does not happen, a dismal future is foreseen – atmospheric pollution requiring domed cities and artificial food production due to pollution of the soil and oceans. A move away from the shopping malls and a return to a more natural way of living for ourselves and our children is our best course for an optimal future (see Postscript).

We are not alone!

Future visions of the Earth in the next 200 years report space stations, colonization of other planets, many similar in environment to Earth, and contact with friendly, more advanced aliens.

Another surprising revelation is that man's evolution is being closely watched by more highly evolved extra-terrestrials in the material universe, and also by higher beings in the spiritual realm – and it is being assessed *not* according to our technological, intellectual or physical development, but according to our spiritual development – the universality of our compassion. Greater interest from these 'Watchers' occurred after the use of atomic bombs to end WW2. The Watchers also seem to be responsible for the barrage of warnings coming through from the 'other side.' These appear to have been successful as the worst possible future, nuclear war (WW3), has not occurred in the prophesized timeframe.

NDErs also provide an answer to the question many of us ask: Why doesn't God step in? Mankind has been allowed free will. Much as animals being filmed in the wild are allowed to follow the 'law of the jungle' without interference from observers, humankind has been allowed to follow its own nature. However, it seems that more spiritually evolved beings have been incarnating in the years since our development of weapons of mass destruction to help mankind get back on track. We are already seeing extraordinary people and communities, at all levels, working to raise consciousness of humanitarian issues and brotherhood.

Our destiny

There is a consensus that a 'golden age,' a new era of peace and brotherhood will come after a 'change in consciousness,' i.e. a worldwide shift in values. There is a strong message that our destiny is unity – a 'consciousness' of the oneness of all creation. This destiny will be forced upon us by catastrophe (all mankind, no matter what their differences, pulling together to survive); however, it is still within our power to step up our humanitarian efforts and achieve it voluntarily.

Part of this destiny is all of us generally becoming more aware of our spiritual nature and existence beyond the physical, which will change beliefs about the limitations of matter, death and religion. Humans will become telepathic, able to communicate with those who have passed over, and knowledge will be available through direct communication with the Source/ God.

This evolution of consciousness will affect the evolution of the human body, which will evolve to become less dense and 'lighter' in terms of mass and construction – and perhaps androgynous. In about 1000 years, possibly sooner, it appears that a new species, *Homo luminous* – 'enlightened man,' will prevail. Humankind will be multi-dimensional, more spirit than flesh, have greatly enhanced mind powers, and be at peace.

We can bring an optimal future closer

While it is interesting to know what we could become, of more immediate concern is the world we are leaving to our children and grandchildren – it will also most likely be the world that we will be reborn into – as it is only too apparent that we are not yet on an optimal timeline.

An important revelation is that our global future hinges on small **individual** actions. Like stones thrown into a pond, every action causes a ripple in the universal consciousness and affects not only the quality of our individual future lives but the timeline of humanity as a whole. Every time we focus on unity and brotherhood rather than diversity, fear and competition; help and share with someone less fortunate; and consciously choose to conserve rather than consume our natural resources, we put ourselves in line, literally, for a better future next time around. In the light of the sometimes strange revelations presented in this study, preparing for the future is not so much about filling the pantry as filling the heart.

RECOMMENDED READING

Regression/ Progression

- *Past Lives, Future Lives* – Jenny Cockell (1996)
- *Same Soul, Many Bodies* – *Discover the healing power of future lives through progression therapy,* Brian Weiss MD (2004)
- *The Future is Yours* – *Introducing future-life progression, the dynamic technique that reveals your destiny,* Anne Jirsch and Monica Cafferky (2007)
- *Anne Jirsch's website –* **www.futurelifeprogression.com** where you can read about others' future-life progressions and download her guided visualization to take you 100 years into the future:

NDEs

All of the books below were written by NDErs, people who were pronounced clinically dead, but who returned to life with memories of an amazing afterlife experience and revelations from one or more spiritual beings. Each has a different perspective that adds to our understanding of the phenomenon.

- *Journey Through the Light and Back* – Mellen-Thomas Benedict (1982), see Kevin Williams' website below
- *Saved by the Light* – *The true story of a man who died twice and the profound revelations he received* – Dannion Brinkley with Paul Perry (1994)
- *At Peace in the Light* – Dannion Brinkley with Paul Perry (1995)
- *Secrets of the Light* – *Lessons from heaven,* Dannion Brinkley and Kathryn Brinkley (2008)
- *Embraced by the Light* – *What happens when you die?* Betty J Eadie (1992)
- *Fast Lane to Heaven* – *a life-after-death journey,* Ned Dougherty (2001)
- *My Descent into Death* – *A second chance at life,* Howard Storm (2005)

- ***Dying to be Me*** *– My journey from cancer, to near death, to true healing,* Anita Moorjani (2012)
- ***To Heaven and Back*** *– A doctor's extraordinary account of her death, heaven, angels and life again,* Mary C. Neal, M.D., (2012)

Research into NDEs

- ***Life After Life*** *– The investigation of a phenomenon: survival of bodily death,* Raymond Moody, M.D., (1975) – a classic. Moody has also written several intriguing books on his subsequent research
- ***Heading Toward Omega*** *– In search of the meaning of the near-death experience,* Kenneth Ring, Ph.D., (1984). Contains an excellent and uplifting chapter on Planetary Visions
- ***Evidence of the Afterlife*** – Jeffrey Long, M.D., with Paul Perry (2010)
- ***Kevin Williams' website*** **–**
  www.near-death.com/experiences/research32
  This is a fascinating website with a staggering range of information on NDEs and related topics.

Other

- ***The Game of Life*** *and how to play it* – Florence Scovel Shinn (first published in 1925 – highly recommended.)
- ***Voyages into the Afterlife*** – Bruce Moen (1999)
- ***Hidden Messages in Water*** – Masaru Emoto (2005)

POSTSCRIPT: AN OPTIMISTIC FUTURE

NDEr Howard Storm asked the 'light beings' he encountered on the other side about where the world would be in an optimistic future **if the desired changes were to take place**. He imagined a space-age technology, but the future he was shown was just the opposite – a return to nature. While the description below is the future Storm was shown, a number of sources agree that **this *could be* what the world is like in 200 years** (by 2200):

- A spiritual reformation and new consciousness of love and harmony has taken place – there is no anxiety, hatred, competition or conflict; instead trust and mutual respect
- No technology because there is no need for devices as humans have the power to control matter and energy
- People live in small communities all over the world, each with its own culture and language, but all people will be able to communicate telepathically
- People are fulfilled and happy where they are so have no need to take vacations, but they may travel to other communities to experience a different culture or environment
- People also communicate telepathically with intelligent beings on other worlds. Life experiences can be shared across galaxies without the need for space travel
- People don't make any distinction between work and play
- Everyone participates in child-rearing as the most important activity of their lives. Most of their time is spent teaching children about love and the wonders of the natural world
- People raise food by sitting next to plants and communing with them, producing mature fruits and vegetables in a few minutes, which they eat fresh. (This is reminiscent of the Findhorn community, a current-day spiritual movement that started 50 years ago in Scotland with the vision of creating a sustainable future for humanity and the planet. At one

time, its impossibly large vegetables – grown through prayer – were legendary)

- The climate is regulated by the collective will of humankind
- If anyone becomes sick or troubled, people gather around, and through prayer, touch and meditation the disease will be cured
- Animals live in harmony with humans
- In the community Storm was shown, inhabitants are wearing clothing similar to Native American dress, with exotic ornaments
- There are no possessions; people seek the welfare of their community
- People understand that their life is a gift from God and value the experience
- When a person is satisfied they have had all the life experience they need, the community gathers around and rejoices while the person lies down and releases his spirit to heaven
- People possess an awareness of God, love and themselves as a part of a vastly greater reality than that which we currently know.

Printed in Poland
by Amazon Fulfillment
Poland Sp. z o.o., Wrocław